BrightRED Study Guide

CfE HIGHER

COMPUTING SCIENCE

Alan Williams

First published in 2014 by:
Bright Red Publishing Ltd
1 Torphichen Street
Edinburgh
EH3 8HX

New edition first published in 2018

A CIP record for this book is available from the British Library.

ISBN 978-1-84948-325-4

With thanks to:
PDQ Digital Media Solutions Ltd, Bungay (layout), Ivor Normand (editorial).
Cover design and series book design by Caleb Rutherford – e i d e t i c.

Acknowledgements
Every effort has been made to seek all copyright-holders. If any have been overlooked,
then Bright Red Publishing will be delighted to make the necessary arrangements.

Permission has been sought from all relevant copyright holders and Bright Red Publishing
are grateful for the use of the following:

Images licensed by Ingram Image (pp 15, 19, 25, 28, 29, 45, 54, 55, 76 & 98); Lilyana Vynogradova/Shutterstock.com
(p 6); Andrey_Popov/Shutterstock.com (p 8); vierdrie/freeimages.com (p 12); Matthew Egginton/Shutterstock.com
(p 16); Tyler Nix/Unsplash (p 19); Filios Sazeides/Unsplash (p 20); Marco Verch/Creative Commons (CC BY 2.0)1
(p 21); ADDRicky/iStock.com (p 23); Alexander Mils/Unsplash (p 24); QUEEN YUNA (CC BY-ND 2.0)3 (p 26);
vasse nicolas, Antoine, (CC BY 2.0)1 (p 27); Cover of Cake Craft & Decoration Magazine © Anglo American Media Ltd
(p 32); cstrom/Creative Commons (CC BY-SA 2.0)2 (p 33); Caleb Rutherford (p 34); (Mick Baker) rooster (CC BY-ND 2.0)3
(p 34); Alvaro Reyes/Unsplash (p 36); Garsya/Shutterstock.com (p 38); Caleb Rutherford (p 40); By George Shaw on
rawpixels/Creative Commons (CC BY-SA 2.0)2 (p 42); lonniehb/freeimages.com (p 42); Douglas Woods (CC BY 2.0)1
(p 47); rawartistsmedia (CC BY-ND 2.0)3 (p 58); NTNU Trondheim (CC BY-SA 2.0)2 (p 58); rawartistsmedia (CC BY-ND
2.0)3 (p 58); David Robert Bliwas (CC BY 2.0)1 (p 58); CaptainIFR/iStock.com (p 64); Bruce Christianson/Unsplash (p 67);
Michael Sum/Unsplash (p 67); Apple and Pear Australia Ltd/Creative Commons (CC BY 2.0)1 (p 69); Benjamint444/
Creative Commons (CC BY-SA 3.0)4 (p 69); Hugowolf/Creative Commons (CC BY-SA 3.0)4 (p 69); Andris Romanovskis/
Unsplash (p 70); James Drury (CC BY 2.0)1 (p 72); pipp/freeimages.com (p 73); Caleb Rutherford (p 74); Windows 8
Release Preview Start Screen used with permission from Microsoft (p 75); style-photographs/iStock.com (p 80);
Qwasyx/iStock.com (p 83).

1 (CC BY 2.0)   http://creativecommons.org/licenses/by/2.0/
2 (CC BY-SA 2.0)   http://creativecommons.org/licenses/by-sa/2.0/
3 (CC BY-ND 2.0)   http://creativecommons.org/licenses/by-nd/2.0/
4 (CC BY-SA 3.0)   http://creativecommons.org/licenses/by-sa/3.0/

Printed and bound in the UK.

CONTENTS

THE HIGHER COURSE

SYLLABUS AND ASSESSMENT

SYLLABUS

This course has four areas of study: Software Design and Development; Computer Systems; Database Design and Development; Web Design and Development.

Software Design and Development	
Development methodologies	• Iterative development process, agile methodologies
Analysis	• Purpose, scope, boundaries • Inputs, processes, outputs
Design	• User design using wireframe • Structure diagrams • Pseudocode • Top-level design • Data flow
Implementation (data types and structures)	• Data types and structures • Parallel 1-D arrays, records, arrays of records
Implementation (computational constructs)	• Parameter passing (formal and actual) • Local and global variables • Subprograms/subroutines, functions, procedures • Pre-defined functions: substrings, conversion between character and ASCII, Mod, Int • Sequential files: open, create, read, write, close • Txt files, CSV files
Implementation	• Standard algorithms using 1-D arrays or arrays of records • Linear search, Find minimum and maximum, Count occurrences
Testing	• Comprehensive final test plan • Types of errors: syntax, execution, logic • De-bugging techniques: dry runs, trace tables, breakpoints, watchpoints
Evaluation	• Fitness for purpose • Efficient use of coding constructs • Usability, maintainability, robustness

Computer Systems	
Data representation	• Two's complement • Floating-point numbers • The range and precision of floating-point numbers • Unicode • Comparison of Unicode with Extended ASCII code • Comparison of bit-mapped and vector graphics
Computer structure	• The fetch–execute cycle • Factors affecting computer system performance: number of processors (cores), width of data bus, cache memory, clock speed
Environmental impact	• The environmental impact of intelligent systems • Heating systems, traffic control, car management systems
Security risks and precautions	• The Computer Misuse Act 1990, unauthorised access, intent to commit a further offence, modification data • Tracking cookies • DOS (denial-of-service) attacks: symptoms, effects, costs, type of fault, reasons • Encryption: public and private keys, digital certificates, digital signatures

contd

Database Design and Development	
Analysis	• Identify end-user and functional requirements
Design	• Entity-relationship diagrams: entity name, attributes, name of relationship • Cardinality of relationship • Entity-occurrence diagram • Compound key • Data dictionary: entity name, attribute name, primary and foreign key • Attribute type: text, number, date, time, Boolean • Attribute size • Validation: presence-check, restricted choice, field length, range • Query design: tables and queries, fields, search criteria, sort order, calculations, grouping
Implementation	• SQL (Structured Query Language): UPDATE, SELECT, DELETE, INSERT • Wildcards • Aggregate functions (MIN, MAX, AVG, SUM, COUNT) • Calculated values, alias • GROUP BY, ORDER BY, WHERE
Testing	• Describe testing • SQL operations work correctly
Evaluation	• Fitness for purpose • Accuracy of output

Web Design and Development	
Analysis	• Identify end-user and functional requirements
Design	• Multi-level website • Effective user interface for user and device type • Design (visual layout and readability) using wireframe • Horizontal navigational bar • Relative positioning of the media • Form inputs • File formats of the media (text, graphics, video, and audio) • Prototyping (low fidelity) from wireframe design
Implementation (CSS)	• Inline, internal and external Cascading Style Sheets (CSS) • Grouping and descendant selectors: display (block, inline, none), float (left, right), clear (both), margins/padding, sizes (height, width) • Create horizontal navigation bars, hover
Implementation (HTML)	• HTML code: nav, header, footer, section, main, form, ID attribute • Form element: input, text, number, textarea, radio, submit • Form element: select • Form data validation: length, presence, range
Implementation (Javascript)	• Javascript mouse event: onmouseover, onmouseout, onclick
Testing	• Usability testing using personas, test cases and scenarios based on low-fidelity prototypes • Input validation works correctly • Navigational bar works correctly • Media content displays correctly • Compatibility testing including: device type (tablet, smartphone, desktop), browser
Evaluation	• Fitness for purpose • Usability

ONLINE

This book is supported by the Bright Red Digital Zone. Visit http://www. brightredbooks.net/ Account/Logon to create an account.

DON'T FORGET

You should use the syllabus as a kind of checklist to make sure that you understand exactly what knowledge is required for assessments in this course. Read it through and ask yourself if you know the topics covered in the table.

DON'T FORGET

In addition to your performance in the exam, your course assessment also includes an assignment practical task. The assignment makes up 50 out of the total 160 marks awarded for the course.

THINGS TO DO AND THINK ABOUT

There is an SQA document called "Higher Course Specification" which you can get from your teacher or download from the Computing Science section of the SQA website. Use this document to study the course content, and in particular use the twelve appendices for further clarification and detailed explanation.

DEVELOPMENT METHODOLOGIES

INTRODUCTION

When writing the short programs required for this course, it is possible to proceed with producing the software without spending too much time on planning. However, in a large-scale commercial project involving teams of programmers, meetings with clients and generating vast amounts of documentation, it is essential that the process be planned.

A software-development methodology is a framework that is used to structure, plan and control the process of developing a software project. Most development methodologies have an overall theme which involves a suite of techniques rather than one principle.

There are many methodologies for software development, but in this course you are only expected to know these two:

1 Iterative development process

2 Agile development methodology

These methodologies have similarities and differences, and each has a different emphasis on aspects of the development process such as team working and client involvement. The purpose of this topic is to understand why agile development is an improvement on an iterative approach to software development, and to understand why it can lead to an approved solution that is developed more efficiently and which better meets the clients' requirements.

ITERATIVE DEVELOPMENT PROCESS

Iterative development proceeds through a series of phases which starts with involving the client at the analysis stage. The developers then proceed through the stages of design, implementation, testing, documentation, evaluation and maintenance.

After the analysis stage, the client is only involved again when evaluating the software to see if the final software system meets the specification that had been agreed at the analysis stage. Very often, the lack of client feedback and flexibility in this type of development results in a product that is not fit for purpose.

In iterative development, the client does not have an opportunity to try out the system and give feedback as it is being developed. Therefore, problems with the usability and functionality of the software can only be identified by the developers, who are not the people who are actually going to use the system. A software system will only be successful if it meets the requirements of the end user.

DON'T FORGET

The iterative software-development process is often called the Waterfall model of software development, since progress starts with analysis and then proceeds through a series of phases in one direction like a cascade of events.

AGILE METHODOLOGIES

Agile software development is a methodology that anticipates the need for flexibility and regular adaptations to changing circumstances. It is a response to the problems that can arise when a large-scale application is delivered at the end of the development process without consulting the client as the project proceeds. The agile methodology focuses on obtaining meaningful feedback from the clients as development proceeds.

Agile development encourages strong teamwork, reduction of excessive documentation and adaptability to changing needs as development proceeds.

Agile development methodologies are commonly used in the development of computer games.

COMPARISON OF ITERATIVE AND AGILE METHODOLOGIES

Make sure that you know which aspects of each development methodology to compare and the differences between them given in this topic.

	Iterative	Agile
Client involvement	A lot of time is spent with the client at the initial analysis stage, after which there is little or no client involvement until the final product is to be evaluated to see if it delivers the agreed specification.	Agile involves regular meetings between the clients and the developers, and necessary changes made to the requirements even late in development. Prototypes can be used to give the clients a hands-on experience during the development, which allows quick action on feedback of any problems.
Teamwork	Team members such as analysts, programmers and testers tend to work in isolation, with little communication between the different development phases.	Most agile teams are located in a shared office space to encourage communication and collaboration. The team will include programmers and the people who manage the project, such as project managers, systems analysts and the clients.
Documentation	There is heavy documentation at each stage of development, which begins with the creation of a lengthy and detailed software specification at the analysis stage.	The emphasis in Agile development is on minimising the amount of documentation to what is seen as absolutely necessary.
Measuring progress	There is a project plan which sets tasks and deadlines which are strictly adhered to.	Agile development focuses on delivering software as quickly as possible and sets short-term development goals called 'sprints' to measure progress.
Adaptability	Iterative development methods are based on the effectiveness of the initial analysis of the proposed project. If circumstances change, then it is difficult to change the direction of the subsequent phases of development.	Agile is a flexible and adaptive methodology which focuses on adapting quickly when the client's needs change during a project.
Testing	Testing is only carried out at the end of the implementation phase once the final software has been produced.	There is no set testing stage. Testing is carried out not at the end of implementation but while the programming is being done.

This table compares the main differences between the two methodologies that are required for this course in terms of client involvement, teamwork, documentation, measuring progress and adaptability.

In particular, research in more detail how the aspects required for this course, such as teamwork and measuring progress, are carried out. For example, there are a range of techniques for measuring progress, and you should try to find at least two of them.

 THINGS TO DO AND THINK ABOUT

Waterfall and Agile are two methodologies for software development. Another commonly used methodology is Rapid Application Development (RAD). Research RAD and compare its advantages and disadvantages with Waterfall and Agile software development.

Try to list two differences between RAD development and Waterfall and Agile development.

Investigate which types of applications are suited to being developed by RAD methodologies rather than Waterfall and Agile development.

 DON'T FORGET

The point of this topic is not just to be able to describe the principles of Iterative and Agile software development but also to compare and contrast these two methodologies in terms of client interaction, teamwork, adaptability etc.

 ONLINE

Visit the website www.versionone.com/agile-101/agile-methodologies to learn more about the techniques and advantages of the agile software development methodology.

 ONLINE TEST

Take the test on Development Methodologies at www.brightredbooks.net

ANALYSIS

INTRODUCTION

The development of a large-scale software project proceeds through several phases. The phases are: analysis, design, implementation, testing, documentation, evaluation and finally maintenance.

Analysis → Design → Implementation → Testing → Documentation → Evaluation → Maintenance

ONLINE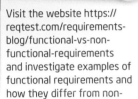

Visit the website https://reqtest.com/requirements-blog/functional-vs-non-functional-requirements and investigate examples of functional requirements and how they differ from non-functional requirements.

The software-development process is often described as the software-development life cycle because, once a system has been developed, there will have to be a regeneration of the process to meet future needs, and in a sense the system is reborn.

For example, a school-reports program may need to be amended in the future to include extra subjects and to generate summaries of marks over the school year. This would involve a repeat of the analysis of the system to identify the school's new requirements, which would then proceed through design and implementation to produce the new program. The updated system would then continue through testing, documentation, evaluation and maintenance to incorporate the new requirements into these stages. The stages of software development can be repeated many times for a system as the client's needs evolve in the future and the life cycle is repeated to meet these requirements.

THE ANALYSIS STAGE

Software development begins with an analysis of the problem that is to be solved.

It is important that the needs of the client are clearly identified at this stage, otherwise time and money will be wasted at future stages in correcting mistakes in a system that does not do what it is supposed to do. In large organisations with complex systems, the analysis stage can take many months to complete.

At one time, the analysis was carried out by programmers who had very good technical skills but were not necessarily good at identifying and describing the client's needs. Nowadays, this stage is carried out by a systems analyst, who should have good technical skills as well as good communication skills.

After the meetings with the client, the purpose of the software and the functional requirements of the software will be specified in detailed documents.

The "purpose of the software" is a description of what the software is to be used for.

Functional Requirements

The functional requirements is a specification of the inputs, processes and outputs that are to be performed by the features and functions of the software.

DON'T FORGET

The purpose of the analysis stage in software development is to give a clear and detailed description of the requirements of the solution. It is not about designing or writing code but purely a logical description of what is required to be done and not how it is to be solved.

Example 1:

The purpose of a program is to enter the title and the number of hits received for each page of a website. It then calculates the average number of hits and finds which pages have received above the average number of hits. It then displays a list of which pages received more than the average number of hits.

The functional requirements of this program in terms of input, processing and output are:

Inputs   Web-page titles, Number of hits
Processes   Calculate average hits, Find the web pages with above the average
Outputs   Web pages with more than the average hits

contd

Example 2:

The purpose of a program is to enter the name, age and species of any pet and then to calculate the age of the pet in human years. The age entered for the pet must be in a valid range for the species.

The program should output the name of the pet and its age in human years.

Functional requirements

Inputs   Pet name, Pet age, Pet species

Processes   Validate age, Calculate human age

Outputs   Pet name, Human age

SCOPE AND BOUNDARIES

It is necessary to clarify and contain a problem by stating the scope and boundaries of the problem before proceeding to the design and implementation stages.

Scope is what the solution needs to do to deliver the project, whereas boundaries is the limit of what it needs to do. The solution is not required to perform tasks that are beyond the boundaries.

Scope

The scope specifies the items that the project will deliver to the client.

For example, this will include items such as the program design, the final program, a test plan with test results etc. It can also include any time limits for the project.

Boundaries

The boundaries are the limits that define what is in the project and what is not in the project. They clarify any assumptions made by the software developers regarding the client's requirements by putting limits on what is to be done.

For example, this will include a clarification of how many items of data are to be input/output, the validation limits for a range-check, the maximum number of fields in a record data structure etc.

 ONLINE

Take the test on Analysis at www.brightredbooks.net

THINGS TO DO AND THINK ABOUT

There has been a pattern in assignments at National 5 level to ask for the end-user and functional requirements of a problem from a brief description. It is likely that this will continue at Higher level, so look at the specimen assignment task for the Higher course and investigate any questions regarding end-user and functional requirements.

Ask your teacher for a copy of the specimen assignment task for Higher Computing Science, and look at Task 3: web design and development.

Try question 3(a), which asks you to "State two end-user requirements and one functional requirement for the website", and ask your teacher for feedback on your answer.

DESIGN

INTRODUCTION

There are three main stages to the design of the software: design of the user interface; design of the structure of the software; design of the detailed logic of the software.

ONLINE

Visit the website www.slideshare.net/piksels/introduction-to-wireframes-presentation for further information and examples of how wireframes are used in software design.

WIREFRAME

A wireframe can be used to represent a design of the program's user interface.

A skeletal outline of the components of the interface is sketched which illustrates the relative positioning of the input and output components used by the program.

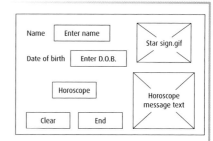

Wireframes can be hand-drawn sketches on paper, or can be done with software that allows them to be created electronically using drawing tools and templates.

STRUCTURE DIAGRAMS

DON'T FORGET

A wireframe is a diagram used to design the program interface, whereas structure diagrams, pseudocode and data-flow diagrams are used to design the structure and processing of the program code.

A structure diagram illustrates how a program is divided up into smaller parts in a series of steps of refinement.

Stepwise Refinement

This is the process of repeatedly breaking down larger, difficult problems step by step into smaller and smaller, easier-to-solve problems.

It is easier for a human being to solve a series of small problems than a large and difficult problem. "Divide and conquer" is a well-known phrase to describe this process.

Stepwise refinement is sometimes called top-down design, for the obvious reason that you start the process at the top, with the problem as a whole, and work downwards in steps of refinement.

Top-Level Design

DON'T FORGET

A structure diagram is more than a picture of boxes showing the parts of a program. It is a common mistake not to think of it as a hierarchy where each level is a refinement of the level above.

A structure diagram starts with the top level of the program and decomposes the program in a series of steps into smaller and smaller blocks.

Different symbols are used in a structure diagram, like so:

- a module requiring further refinement
- selection
- repetition
- a statement requiring no further refinement

Example:

A structure diagram representing the calculation of the average of a list of exam marks:

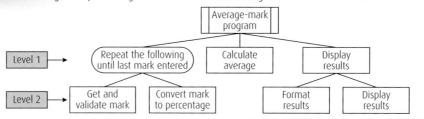

PSEUDOCODE

Pseudocode is used at the design stage to give the detailed logic of the program code.

Three features of pseudocode are:

1   It describes the detailed logic of a program without having to bother about the details of how it is going to be implemented in the chosen programming language.

2   It shows the control constructs of the algorithm, i.e. looping, branching etc.

3   It shows the stepwise refinement of the problem in levels of decomposition.

Level 1

1   Get Mark
2   Find Grade
3   Display Grade

Level 2

1.1   DO
1.2   RECEIVE Mark FROM KEYBOARD
1.3   IF Mark < 0 OR Mark > 100 THEN
1.4   SEND ["Error. Not possible!"] TO DISPLAY
1.5   END IF
1.6   UNTIL Mark >= 0 AND Mark <= 100
2.1   SELECT CASE Mark
2.2   CASE Mark >= 70
2.3   SET Grade TO "A"
2.4   CASE Mark 60 TO 69
2.5   SET Grade TO "B"
2.6   CASE Mark 50 TO 59
2.7   SET Grade TO "C"
2.8   CASE Mark 0 TO 49
2.9   SET Grade TO "FAIL"
2.10 END SELECT
3.1   FORMAT Grade
3.2   SEND ["The grade was: ", Grade] TO DISPLAY

DON'T FORGET

Don't use programming keywords in pseudocode, e.g. Age = Inputbox("Enter an age.").

Use ordinary English, such as RECEIVE Age FROM KEYBOARD.

DATA FLOW

Part of the design of the structure of a program is to list the subprograms and to detail which parameters require to be passed in and out from each subprogram.

Example:

A program enters the radius and height of a cylinder.
The program then calculates the volume and surface area and then displays the radius, height, volume and surface area.

The top-level algorithm is:	Parameters In	Parameters Out
1 Enter radius and height	Radius, Height	Radius, Height
2 Calculate the volume and area	Radius, Height, Volume, Area	Volume, Area
3 Display radius, height, volume and surface	Radius, Height, Volume, Area	

ONLINE

Take the test on Design at www.brightredbooks.net

💭 THINGS TO DO AND THINK ABOUT

Study the Higher Course Specification document, Appendix 3, which has examples of software-design techniques including pseudocode, structure charts, data flow and refinement.

IMPLEMENTATION (DATA TYPES)

INTRODUCTION

Programs need to be able to store text, whole numbers, decimal numbers and so on. Data types are used to store different types of data within a program.

In this course, you need to know about String, Character, Integer, Real and Boolean data types.

Each data type is stored differently in main memory. For example, a programming language might store an integer in a 32-bit two's complement notation, while a real data type is stored as a floating-point number with a 32-bit mantissa and a 16-bit exponent. Declaring a variable as a specific data type allows the translator to allocate memory to store the program's variable. It also restricts the range of operations which can be performed on any given type, and helps the programmer to avoid making silly mistakes such as trying to multiply two letters together.

ONLINE

Enter the text "Visual Basic data type summary" into a search engine to further explore the range of data types available in the Visual Basic programming language. Do the same search for the Python programming language.

STRING

A string data type is used to store an item of text and a sequence of characters.

This data type would be used to store a colour, the name of a pet, a question in a quiz and so on.

String data is enclosed in quotation marks to let the program know that it is not a number but an item of text.

For example, "Paris", "hockey", "rose petal", "What is the height of King Kong?" etc. should be stored in a string data type.

DON'T FORGET

Typically, programmers must enclose text in quotation marks for the data to be recognised as a string and not a number. For example, to assign the string variable Country to Iceland requires the instruction: Country = "Iceland" and not Country = Iceland.

CHARACTER

Some languages have a character data type, which is used to store a single character.

This data type could be used to store "M" or "F" for the sex of a person.

For example, "T", "F", "H" or "L" should be stored in a character data type.

INTEGER

An integer data type is used to store positive and negative whole numbers, and zero.

This data type would be used to store the score when throwing a die, the number of students in a school, winning lottery numbers and so on.

For example, 7, 80, −20, 0, −57 or 702 should be stored in an integer data type.

REAL

A real data type is used to store positive and negative decimal or fractional numbers.

This data type can be used to store the height of a girl in metres, the winning time for a 100 metres race, the weight in kg of a melon and so on.

For example, 2·5, 3·14, −6·57, 25·0 or −400·783 should be stored in a real data type.

BOOLEAN

A Boolean variable is used to store only two values: True and False. This data type would be used to store the answer to a "true or false?" question: whether someone is married or not, whether a number entered into a program is valid or not, and so on.

	True	False
Five spiders have more legs than seven wasps?	☐	☐

DON'T FORGET

The data type Boolean should have a capital letter, because it is named after the British mathematician George Boole, who helped to establish modern algebra of logic.

DECLARING VARIABLES

Most programming languages require variables to be declared before they are used and assigned values.

The variables are declared with a statement that gives the variable a name and states its data type.

Example in Visual Basic
Dim MyName As String
Dim Sex As Char
Dim ExamMark As Integer
Dim Average As Single
Dim Found As Boolean

VIDEO LINK

Learn more about data types by watching the clip at www.brightredbooks.net

Example:

The program below is written in SQA reference language. It stores the names of eight athletes, their best 100 metres time to the nearest tenth of a second, and their sex. The program searches for a time entered by the user and returns the name, time and sex of the athlete, or gives a message if the time was not found. This program uses the following data types:

```
1   SET Athletes TO ["Peter", "Polly", "Patrick", "Paul", "Penelope", "Philip", "Priscilla", "Phoebe"]
2   SET Times TO [10·1, 11·3, 10·5, 9·8, 12·1, 10·2, 10·8, 11·3]
3   SET Sexes TO ["M", "F", "M", "M", "F", "M", "F", "F"]
4   SET Found TO FALSE
5   SET Position TO 0
6   RECEIVE SearchTime FROM KEYBOARD
7   REPEAT
8        IF Times(Position) = SearchTime THEN
9            SET Found TO TRUE
10       ELSE
11           SET Position TO Position + 1
12       END IF
13   UNTIL (Found = TRUE) OR (Position = 8)
14   IF Found = TRUE THEN
15       SEND ["Athlete: ", Athletes(Position)] TO DISPLAY
16       SEND ["Time: ", Times(Position)] TO DISPLAY
17       SEND ["Sex: ", Sexes(Position)] TO DISPLAY
18   ELSE
19       SEND ["The time you entered was not found."] TO DISPLAY
20   END IF
```

Variable	Data Type
Athletes	STRING
Times	REAL
Sexes	CHARACTER
Found	BOOLEAN
Position	INTEGER
SearchTime	REAL

THINGS TO DO AND THINK ABOUT

Programming languages have a variety of data types. When you are coding your own programs in your practical work, think carefully about the variables required to store your program's data, and declare them with the correct data type.

Ask your teacher for a copy of the specimen assignment task for Higher Computing Science, and look at Task 2: software design and development.

Write down the variable and data types required for this program, and ask your teacher for feedback on your answer.

ONLINE TEST

Take the test on Implementation (data types) at www.brightredbooks.net

IMPLEMENTATION (STRUCTURES)

ONLINE

Visit the Wikipedia website at www.wikipedia.org/wiki/Array_data_structure for information on one-dimensional arrays and how data is stored and accessed in them.

DON'T FORGET

In your programming tasks, you should always use an array to store a list of items. The program will be much more efficient than if you store each item in a separate variable.

ONLINE

The BBC Bitesize website has further information on record data types and examples of their use.

Enter the following keywords into a search engine: "bitesize computing science record data type" to explore this topic further.

ONE-DIMENSIONAL (1-D) ARRAYS

An array is used to store a group of data where the data is all of the same data type.

For example, an array could be used to store 20 marks for students in an exam, the names of 60 contacts on a mobile phone, the answer to 40 multiple-choice exam questions, and so on.

Each element of the array is identified by using the array name with an index number in brackets (sometimes called the subscript) of the array.

When an array is declared, its size (or dimension) is stated.

The diagram below represents an array called "Dwarfs", which stores seven strings. This array would be declared with a statement of the form "Dim Dwarfs[6] as String". The "6" in brackets indicates that the highest index in the array is to be 6. This means that this array will store seven items of data, since the first index is zero.

Dwarfs	[0]	[1]	[2]	[3]	[4]	[5]	[6]
	Dopey	Bashful	Sneezy	Sleepy	Happy	Grumpy	Doc

An element of the "Dwarfs" array can be referred to using the array name with the subscript in index.

Example:

SET Dwarfs[4] TO "Happy"
This statement assigns the string "Happy" to variable number 5 of the array called "Dwarfs".

Dwarfs	[0]	[1]	[2]	[3]	[4]	[5]	[6]
					Happy		

RECORD DATA TYPE

A record data type is a data structure which can store variables of different data types in fields.

It provides a means of collecting together a set of different data types into one named structure.

When performing operations such as sorting, a record data structure is preferable to using a number of parallel 1-D arrays, where there is no built-in link between the arrays, and the array indices may become unsynchronised. All the data in the fields of a record are moved together as a unit.

For example, the definition shown below creates a record data type called "Students" using a Type statement.

Type Student
    FirstName As String
    Surname As String
    Sex As Char
    Height As Single
    Exam As Integer
End Type

Arrays of Records

An array of the Student data type can then be declared to store a group of records.

Each record is identified by an index just like any array.

For example, Dim Students[59] As Student

contd

This array stores 60 student records, the first record being Students(0) and the last record being Students(59)

The following example uses the SQA reference language that will be used in exams and assessments for coding questions involving record data structures.

Example:

The table below contains details on 10 pets.

Name	Species	Age	Weight_kg
Rocky	Dog	5	29·3
Vegas	Cat	8	4·3
Humpy	Rabbit	3	1·2
Blackie	Dog	16	21·7
Snowy	Dog	1	43·5
Baskerville	Dog	13	38·5
Princess	Cat	15	3·7
Pickles	Dog	9	16·8
Samantha	Cat	4	2·9
Einstein	Dog	7	18·6

A record data structure can be declared to store the details for one pet by specifying the fields and the data type of each field in the record.

Record Pet IS {STRING Name, STRING Species, INTEGER Age, SINGLE Weight_kg}

An array of MyPets records can then be declared to store the record details for 10 pets:

DECLARE MyPets[9] AS ARRAY OF Pet

Each record is identified by an index just like any array.
i.e. MyPets[0], MyPets[1], MyPets[2] etc.

The following statements populate the first two records of the array with values:

SET MyPets[0] TO ("Rocky", "Dog", 5, 29·3)
SET MyPets[1] TO ("Vegas", "Cat", 8, 4·3)

The following pseudocode counts the number of dogs that are heavier than a value entered by the user from the keyboard.

Each field in a record is identified with a dot notation.

i.e. MyPets[Index]. Name, MyPets[Index].Species etc.

```
SET Count TO 0
RECEIVE Weight from KEYBOARD
FOR Index FROM 0 TO 9 DO
    IF MyPets[Index].Species = "Dog" AND
        MyPets[Index].Weight_kg > Weight THEN
            SET Count TO Count + 1
    END IF
END FOR
SEND ["The count is: ", Count] TO DISPLAY
```

 **DON'T FORGET**

Exam questions on record data structures will use the SQA reference language shown in the example here. However, you can use the coding from a programming language of your choice when writing your own code to answer questions.

 **ONLINE TEST**

Take the test on Implementation (structures) at www.brightredbooks.net

 ## THINGS TO DO AND THINK ABOUT

Investigate the data structures available in the programming language that you use for your practical work in this course.

Find out how your language is used to declare the record data structure "Pet" used in this spread, and then write code to declare an array of 10 pet records.

IMPLEMENTATION (CONSTRUCTS) 1

SCOPE OF VARIABLES

The aim in good programming is to limit the scope of program variables as far as possible. This means that the effect of any changes to the variable during modifications to the program need only be traced through a part of the program and not the whole program.

Local Variables

A local variable only exists within the subprogram in which it is declared.

It can only be changed within that subprogram and will not be recognised by any other subprogram.

Global Variables

A global variable is recognised by all the subprograms within the program.

It can be changed by any subprogram in the program.

The aim is to minimise the number of global variables, since any change to a global variable in one subprogram must be traced through every other subprogram.

SUBPROGRAMS

Procedures

A procedure produces an effect, e.g. sorting a list of marks, displaying a menu and so on.

Shown below is the definition of a procedure which calculates the perimeter and area of a rectangle and displays the results.

```
Sub RectangleFacts(Length, Breadth)
'This procedure finds the perimeter and area of a rectangle and displays the results
Dim Perimeter As Single
Dim Area As Single
Let Perimeter = 2 * (Length + Breadth)
Let Area = Length * Breadth
Picture1.Print "The perimeter of the rectangle is " & Perimeter
Picture1.Print "The area of the rectangle is " & Area
End Sub
```

The procedure is then used in a program with statements such as:

"Call RectangleFacts(L, B)"; "Call RectangleFacts(3, 8)" and so on.

Functions

A function returns a single value, e.g. returning the mode of an array of numbers, returning the number of vowels in a string, and so on.

Shown below is the definition of a function to return the maximum value in an integer array.

```
Function Max(Scores() As Integer) As Integer
'This function returns the highest value in an array of integers.
Let Max = Scores(0)
For i = 1 To 9
```

contd

```
        If Scores(i) > Max Then
            Let Max = Scores(i)
        End If
    Next i
    End Function
```

The function is then used in the program with statements such as:

```
Let Highest = Max(Numbers())
Picture1.Print "The best mark was " & Max(Marks())
```

DON'T FORGET

In the Area function, the parameters Length and Breadth are both passed by value, since the changes made to the parameters do not have to be passed out.

PARAMETERS

A parameter is a variable or value that is passed into and/or out of a subprogram. There are two types of parameters:

- The formal parameters are used in the subprogram definition
- The actual parameters are passed into the subprogram when the subprogram is called.

DON'T FORGET

The term "argument" is sometimes used to refer to the actual value (also known as the actual parameter) passed to a subprogram when it is used.

PASSING PARAMETERS BY REFERENCE AND BY VALUE

- Passing parameters by reference is used when the value being passed in is to be updated and passed back out again. (The variable itself is passed into the subprogram so that any changes to the variable will change the variable.)

- Passing parameters by value is used when a value is passed into a subprogram but does not require to be passed out. (The subprogram makes a copy of the variable so that any changes to the copy of the variable will not change the variable.)

DON'T FORGET

Arrays are always passed by reference to subprograms, since making a copy of a large data structure such as an array would use up too much memory.

Example

The program shown below asks for the length and breadth of a rectangle and then calculates the area and displays the result.

```
Dim L As Integer
Dim B As Integer

Sub GetSides(ByRef Length As Integer, ByRef Breadth As Integer)
Length = InputBox("Please enter the length of the rectangle.")
Breadth = InputBox("Please enter the breadth of the rectangle.")
End Sub
```

Procedure declaration: Length + Breadth are formal parameters

```
Function Area(ByVal Length As Integer, ByVal Breadth As Integer)
As Integer
Area = Length * Breadth
End Function
```

Function declaration: Length + Breadth are formal parameters

```
Private Sub Command1_Click()
Call GetSides(L, B)
End Sub
```

Function call: L + B are actual parameters

```
Private Sub Command2_Click()
Picture1.Print "The area of the rectangle is " & Area(L, B)
End Sub
```

ONLINE TEST

Take the test on Implementation (constructs) 1 at www.brightredbooks.net

THINGS TO DO AND THINK ABOUT

Study the specimen coursework task and read Task 2: software design and development.

For each of the subprograms in the top-level design, identify whether the subprogram should be a procedure or a function.

IMPLEMENTATION (CONSTRUCTS) 2

ONLINE

Visit the website www.vbtutor.net/lesson13.html for further examples of the Left, Right and Mid substring functions.

PRE-DEFINED FUNCTIONS

A pre-defined function is a function already built into the programming language to perform mathematical calculations, manipulate text, format values etc.

Substrings

The Left, Right and Mid functions are used to return part of a string.

1   Left function
Returns a specified number of characters from the left-hand side of a string.
e.g. Left("Hello world", 4) returns "Hell", and Left(("Hello world", 7) returns "Hello w".

2   Right function
Returns a specified number of characters from the right-hand side of a string.
e.g. Right("Partick Thistle", 2) returns "le", and Right("Partick Thistle", 11) returns "ick Thistle".

3   Mid function
Returns a specified number of characters starting from a specified position in a string.
e.g. If Mystring = "I made him an offer that he could not refuse" then
     Mid(MyString, 1, 5) returns "I mad" (Starting at position 1, returns 5 characters)
     Mid(MyString, 3, 8) returns "made him" (Starting at position 3, returns 8 characters)
     Mid(MyString, 15, 1) returns "o" (Starting at position 15, returns 1 character).

INT function

Most programming languages have an inbuilt Int function that returns the whole part of a decimal number and discards anything after the decimal point.

e.g. The example below assigns 63 to the Weight variable in Visual Basic.
     Weight = 63·738
     Weight = Int(Weight)

Conversion between ASCII and characters

Most programming languages have an inbuilt function to convert a decimal integer into its ASCII equivalent.

Example: Chr(65) = "A"

The reverse operation is an ASCII function which returns the ASCII code of a character.

Example: Asc("A") = 65

MOD operator

The MOD operator returns the remainder after a number is divided by a divisor.

The example below assigns the value 3 to the Answer variable.

(18 divided by 5 has a remainder of 3)

Answer = 18 MOD 5

The example below converts the number of inches stored in a TotalInches variable into feet and inches.

The Feet variable is assigned the value 5, and the Inches variable is assigned the value 7.

e.g. TotalInches = 67
     Feet = Int(TotalInches / 12)
     Inches = TotalInches MOD 12

FILE-HANDLING

A sequential file stores items of data one after another and is terminated with an end-of-file (EOF) marker.

Open/Create

A file must be opened before input and output operations can be performed on it.

Example   OPEN Filename
          CREATE Filename

Close

After it has been opened and read or written to, a file must be closed.

Example   CLOSE Filename

Read

"Read" is the operation where items of data in a file are input into main memory. The example below reads a file into an array with 10 elements.

Example:

```
OPEN Filename
FOR Count FROM 0 TO 9 DO
    RECEIVE Array(Count) FROM Filename
END FOR
CLOSE Filename
```

Write

"Write" is the operation where items of data in main memory are output to a file. The example below writes the items in an array with 20 elements to a file.

Example:

```
OPEN Filename
FOR Count FROM 0 TO 19 DO
    SEND Array(Count) TO Filename
END FOR
CLOSE Filename
```

CSV files (Comma-Separated Values)

A CSV (.csv extension) is a text file containing rows of data with each row containing data items that are separated by commas.

Example:

The details of the exam marks for 20 students in Computing are loaded from a CSV file named Exam_Marks.
Each line of the file contains a Student name and a Computing mark.
Part of the file is shown below.

          Mary Marsbar, 73
          Walter Wigwam, 57
          Penelope Peatbog, 65
          ...

Shown below, in SQA reference language, is code that reads the data from the CSV file into four 1-D arrays.
The 1-D arrays are defined as follows:

```
DECLARE Student[19] AS ARRAY OF STRING
DECLARE Computing[19] AS ARRAY OF INTEGER

OPEN Exam_Marks
    FOR Line FROM 0 TO 19 DO
        FOR EACH Comma Separated Item in Line
            SET Student[Line] TO Comma Separated Item
            SET Computing[Line] TO Comma Separated Item
        NEXT FOR EACH
    NEXT FOR
CLOSE Exam_Marks
```

DON'T FORGET

A user-defined function is a function that has been written and saved by a programmer to be used over and over again in the future. An inbuilt function is a function that is part of the programming language to make it more efficient for the programmer to develop code.

 ONLINE TEST

Take the test on Implementation (constructs) 2 at www.brightredbooks.net

 THINGS TO DO AND THINK ABOUT

The programming language that you use for your practical work will have file-handling operations. Use the language's online help to investigate these operations.

STANDARD ALGORITHMS

LINEAR SEARCH

This code searches for a value at the first item in a list and continues searching through each item of the list in turn.

Example:

```
1 SET Position TO 0
2 RECEIVE SearchValue FROM KEYBOARD
3    REPEAT
4      IF Item(Position) = SearchValue THEN
5        SEND [SearchValue] TO DISPLAY
6      END IF
7      SET Position TO Position + 1
8 UNTIL Position = No of items in list
```

This code is not efficient, since it continues to search to the end of the list even if the search value has been found.

The following improved code makes use of a condition that will stop the search once the search value has been found.

```
1  SET Found TO FALSE
2  SET Position TO 0
3  RECEIVE SearchValue FROM KEYBOARD
4  REPEAT
5      IF Item(Position) = SearchValue THEN
6          SET Found TO TRUE
7          SEND [SearchValue] TO DISPLAY
8      ELSE
9          SET Position TO Position + 1
10     END IF
11 UNTIL (Found = TRUE) OR (Position = No of items in list)
12 IF Found = FALSE THEN
13     SEND ["Message not found."] TO DISPLAY
14 END IF
```

FINDING MAXIMUM

This algorithm is used to find the maximum value in a list:

1 a max variable is set to the first item in the list

2 each item in the list in turn is compared to the max to see if it is bigger

3 every time the item in the list is bigger than the max, the max is updated to that item.

Example:

```
Finding the maximum in a list of items:
1 SET Position TO 0
2 SET Max TO Item(Position)
3 FOR Position FROM 1 TO No of items in list – 1 DO
4     IF Item(Position) > Max THEN
5         SET Max TO Item(Position)
6     END IF
7 END FOR
8 SEND ["The maximum value is", Max] TO DISPLAY
```

FINDING MINIMUM

This algorithm is virtually identical to finding the maximum value, only each item in the list is compared to the min to see if it is smaller.

Example:

Finding the minimum in a list of items:

```
1 SET Position TO 0
2 SET Min TO Item(Position)
3 FOR Position FROM 1 TO No of items in list – 1 DO
4     IF Item(Position) < Min THEN
5         SET Min TO Item(Position)
6     END IF
7 END FOR
8 SEND ["The minimum value is ", Min] TO DISPLAY
```

COUNTING OCCURRENCES

This algorithm counts how often a value entered from the keyboard occurs in a list of items:

1   set a counter to zero

2   search a list for the occurrence of the search value

3   increment the counter by 1 each time the search value is found.

Example:

Counting occurrences of a search value in a list of items:

```
1 SET Count TO 0
2 RECEIVE SearchValue FROM KEYBOARD
3 FOR Position FROM 0 TO No of items in list – 1 DO
4     IF SearchValue = Item(position) THEN
5         SET Count TO Count + 1
6     END IF
7 END FOR
8 SEND [Count] TO DISPLAY
```

Counting occurrences using a record data structure

The following code counts the number of students who passed an exam (pass mark 50) using an array of records as defined below.

Record Student IS {STRING Name, STRING Class, INTEGER ExamMark}
DECLARE Students[19] AS ARRAY OF Student

```
1 SET Passes TO 0
2 FOR Position FROM 0 TO 19 DO
3     IF Students(Position).ExamMark >= 50 THEN
4         SET Passes TO Passes + 1
5     END IF
6 END FOR
7 SEND ["Number of passes ", Passes] TO DISPLAY
```

THINGS TO DO AND THINK ABOUT

The SQA reference language that you have used in the National 5 course has been extended for the Higher course to take account of extra programming features. These extras include the use of record data structures, functions, procedures and file-handling operations.

YouTube is a useful source of video tutorials covering the programming fundamentals that you will meet in this course. Research these programming features by entering keywords such as "tutorial", the language you use for programming, "functions" etc.

TESTING

COMPREHENSIVE FINAL TEST PLAN

A final test plan should be constructed before a program is written.

This is a document that describes the approach and test data that is to be used to test the program.

A mixture of normal, extreme and exceptional data should be used to test the software thoroughly.

Normal data
One set of test data should be chosen to test that the software gives correct results for commonplace data without any unusual or extreme data.

Extreme data
One set of test data should be chosen to see if the software can handle data on the edge or limits.

Exceptional data
One set of test data should be chosen for unusual cases (e.g. invalid inputs) in order to test the robustness of the software.

Example:
A program enters seven exam marks as a percentage. The program then displays the number of marks in each grade (Fail 0...49, C 50...59, B 60...69, A 70...100).

The following sets of data would cover a good range of cases:
Normal test data   Marks 67, 34, 78, 56, 63, 40, 51
Extreme data   Marks 50, 100, 0, 60, 70, 49, 69
Exceptional data   Marks 144, −13, 50·5, 66A, 7000000, A, Polly

SYNTAX, EXECUTION AND LOGIC ERRORS

Syntax Error

Syntax errors are mistakes in the grammar of the programming language. They are reported by the translator program, since they are breaking the rules of the language and can't be translated. Here are some examples of syntax errors:

1   Misspellings of language keywords: e.g. Prnt, Nexy I and so on

2   Missing inverted commas: e.g. Picture1.Print "Hello

3   A For...Next loop with a For but no Next.

Execution Error

These are errors that are not detected by the translator but are discovered when the program is run.

A common execution error occurs when the program is instructed to divide by zero, which generates an error – and the program will crash. Another example is when a program attempts to read data from a file on disc, and the disc is not present in the disc drive. Good software should have error-trapping techniques to avoid these errors.

Execution errors are also known as run-time errors, since they are errors that prevent the instruction from being run.

Logical Error

A program can translate error-free and have no run-time errors but still not give correct results, because of an error in the logic of the instructions – for example, writing code to add two numbers instead of multiplying them, or subtracting two numbers the wrong way around.

DRY RUNS, TRACE TABLES, BREAKPOINTS, WATCHPOINTS

Dry Run

This technique involves stepping through the program instructions and manually working out on paper how the program variables are updated. This involves updating the value of variables, usually in a table, after the execution of each instruction to check that the correct logical steps are being followed by the program code.

Trace Table

A trace is used by a programmer to manually step through the program line by line while watching how variables are updated in a trace table after each instruction has been executed.

Example:

AnnualPay	QuarterlyBonus	Count	Count > 3
35000			
	400		
		0	
35400			
		1	
			False
35800			
		2	
			False
36200			
		3	
			False
36600			
		4	
			True

The trace table above shows how the values of the variables AnnualPay, QuarterlyBonus and the condition Count > 3 are updated when the following code is stepped through one line at a time.

```
SET AnnualPay TO 35000
SET QuarterlyBonus TO 400
SET Count TO 0
REPEAT
    SET AnnualPay TO AnnualPay + QuarterlyBonus
    SET Count TO Count + 1
UNTIL Count > 3
```

Breakpoint

A breakpoint is set as a marker alongside an instruction in the program. When the program reaches the breakpoint, program execution is suspended. The contents of the variables in the program can then be examined, typically by hovering over a variable in the code with the mouse pointer; and a small text box displays the value of the variable.

Watchpoint

A watchpoint is a conditional breakpoint that halts program execution when a condition is met, such as a variable being less than a certain value.

THINGS TO DO AND THINK ABOUT

Explore the software-development tools provided by the programming language that you use. Trace tables and breakpoints are provided with most programming languages.

Open one of the programs that you have created, and insert breakpoints to monitor how the program variables are updated as the program proceeds.

DON'T FORGET

A dry run can be used to locate logical errors in the program, but it will not find syntax errors. It can also help to identify run-time errors such as dividing by zero.

ONLINE

Visit the BBC Bitesize website www.bbc.com/bitesize/guides/zg4j7ty/revision/5 for a more detailed explanation of the difference between breakpoint and watchpoints.

ONLINE TEST

Take the test on Testing at www.brightredbooks.net

EVALUATION

TERMS USED TO EVALUATE SOFTWARE

There are various terms that are used to describe and evaluate computer software. These include "fit for purpose", "efficiency", "usability", "maintainable" and "robust".

FITNESS FOR PURPOSE

Software is fit for purpose if the product is suitable for its intended purpose – that is, if it does what it is supposed to do in terms of the user and functional requirements.

The evaluation should identify any discrepancies between the software specification and the completed software.

EFFICIENT USE OF CODING CONSTRUCTS

It is not efficient to solve a small problem with a very large program. The use of arrays, and then processing the array values in loops, is much more efficient than using many individual variables.

Example 1: Arrays

Two programs each enter five numbers and then calculate and display the average number.

Program A uses an array, which makes the program more efficient than Program B, which does not use an array.

Program A
```
1   SET Total TO 0
2   FOR Position FROM 0 TO 4 DO
3       RECEIVE List_of_numbers(Position) FROM KEYBOARD
4       SET Total TO Total + List_of_numbers(Position)
5   END FOR
6   SEND ["The average is: ", Total / 5] TO DISPLAY
```

Program B
```
1   SET Total TO 0
2   RECEIVE Number1 FROM KEYBOARD
3   SET Total TO Total + Number1
4   RECEIVE Number2 FROM KEYBOARD
5   SET Total TO Total + Number2
6   RECEIVE Number3 FROM KEYBOARD
7   SET Total TO Total + Number3
8   RECEIVE Number4 FROM KEYBOARD
9   SET Total TO Total + Number4
10  RECEIVE Number5 FROM KEYBOARD
11  SET Total TO Total + Number5
12  SEND ["The average is: ", Total / 5] TO DISPLAY
```

Example 2: Nested IFs

Two programs each display the grade awarded to a percentage mark.

Program A uses multiple IFs to solve the problem. This is inefficient because, if the first IF is true, then the remaining IFs are still executed to see if they are true, even though they would not be true.

Program B uses nested IFs, which means that if the first IF is true, then the rest of the code is not executed because it is part of the ELSE.

DON'T FORGET

Software is said to be efficient if its time or storage requirements are in proportion to the scale of the problem. In other words, writing a program to solve a simple problem should not require a large and complex program which takes a long time to run.

DON'T FORGET

The efficiency of code can be improved by using arrays as opposed to separate variables, and using nested IFs as opposed to multiple IFs. These programming features are likely to come up in the exam and the assignment task.

contd

```
Program A                               Program B
If Mark >= 70 Then                      If Mark >= 70 Then
    MsgBox("A pass")                        MsgBox("A pass")
End If                                   Else
If Mark >= 60 And Mark < 70 Then            If Mark >= 60 Then
    MsgBox("B pass")                            MsgBox("B pass")
End If                                       Else
If Mark >= 50 And Mark < 60 Then                If Mark >= 50 Then
    MsgBox("C pass")                                MsgBox("C pass")
End If                                           Else
If Mark < 50 Then                                   MsgBox("Fail") Then
    MsgBox("Fail")                              End If
End If                                       End If
                                        End If
```

USABILITY

Usability is a term to describe how intuitive the software is from a user's point of view. In other words, can the user perform tasks quickly and with few errors?

It is much easier for a user to enter a date by selecting a date from a calendar than entering it as text, where it will probably take longer and be very easy for the user to enter the wrong value or not enter the date in the correct format.

Other ways of improving the usability of software when entering data include:

- Using radio buttons for making selections such as male/female, M/F etc.

- Using drop-down lists to restrict choice for selecting a month, flight departure, airport etc.

- Using predictive text input which predicts the intended text from a small number of key presses and hence speeds up the speed of data entry.

MAINTAINABILITY

Software is maintainable if subsequent modifications can be performed easily to adapt to different circumstances. Two factors that affect maintainability include:

- Readable code, which makes it easy to modify software by using meaningful variable names, comments, indentations and white space

- Independent modules, by using functions and procedures effectively so that changes to one subprogram only affect that subprogram and do not need to be traced through the entire program to see the impact of the changes.

ONLINE

Go online to the website www.usabilityfirst.com/about-usability for more information on software usability and why it is important.

ROBUSTNESS

Software is robust if it does not crash easily with unexpected input. For example, if the user enters a letter when numeric data is expected, the software should not just crash but should give an error message and invite the user to re-enter the data.

Other common ways in which software can unexpectedly crash include:

- Trying to access a file with the wrong pathway.

- Using an index outside the bounds of an array.

 ONLINE TEST

Take the test on Evaluation at www.brightredbooks.net

 THINGS TO DO AND THINK ABOUT

Investigate what features are available on your smartphone or tablet to change the settings for the user interface. These will include accessibility options to improve the usability for disabled users.

REVISION QUESTIONS 1

QUESTION 1

State a term which describes each of the following statements about software.

(a) Software that does not crash easily when given invalid data.

(b) A software-development methodology where active user involvement is imperative to gain feedback.

(c) Software that solves the problem that it is required to solve in terms of usability and functionality requirements.

(d) Software which can be easily adapted to changing requirements in the future.

(e) Software that solves a problem without using an unnecessarily large amount of code.

QUESTION 2

The organisers of an ice-skating competition require a computer program to process the judges' scores and quickly and accurately return the score achieved by each skater.

The program will use an array to store the scores and make use of standard algorithms to process the scores.

Each skater receives a score in the range 0·0–6·0 from each of six judges.

A skater's overall score is calculated from the total of the six scores minus the best and the worst scores.

Judge	1	2	3	4	5	6
Score	5·2	5·5	4·9	5·2	5·7	5·3

Overall score = 5·2 + 5·5 + 4·9 + 5·2 + 5·7 + 5·3 – 5·7 – 4·9 = 21·2.

(a) The program validates each score entered by the judges with a conditional loop.

Explain why a conditional loop is required.

(b) A subroutine called "final_score" calculates the overall score for a skater from the six judges' scores.

State whether the "final_score" subroutine is a procedure or a function, and justify your answer.

(c) The "final_score" subroutine uses an array called "Scores" as an input parameter.

(i) Explain why an integer data type is not suitable for this parameter, and give a suitable data type.

(ii) State whether the "Scores" array should be passed by reference or by value, and explain your answer.

(d) This program could have used six separate variables or a 1-dimensional array to store the judges' scores for an ice-skater.

What are the advantages of a 1-dimensional array over six variables in terms of:

(i) future maintenance

(ii) efficiency

(iii) data storage requirements?

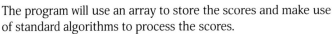

contd

(e) The code below shows a program to calculate the overall score for a skater from the six individual judges' scores. The code is correct but has three incomplete lines.

Complete the code for line 12, line 18 and line 20 of the algorithm.

```
1   SET Scores TO [5·2, 5·5, 4·9, 5·2, 5·7, 5·3]
2   SET Position TO 0
3   SET Min TO Scores[Position]
4   FOR Position FROM 1 TO 5 DO
5       IF Scores[Position] < Min THEN
6           SET Min TO Scores[Position]
7       END IF
8   END FOR
9   SET Position TO 0
10  SET Max TO Score[Position]
11  FOR Position FROM 1 TO 5 DO
12      IF ...
13          SET Max TO Scores[Position]
14      END IF
15  END FOR
16  SET Total TO 0
17  FOR Position FROM 0 TO 5 DO
18      SET Total TO ...
19  END FOR
20  SET Overall TO ...
21  SEND ["The overall score is: ", Overall] TO DISPLAY
```

DON'T FORGET

This question makes use of the finding maximum and finding minimum standard algorithms. These are very similar algorithms and only vary in that the ">" comparison is used in the maximum code and the "<" comparison is used in the minimum code – and of course the variable names must change, or the code would not be very readable!

QUESTION 3

Wendy works as a programmer in the film industry. She is creating an app with details of Oscar winners since they started in 1927. Users of the app can search for Oscar winners by year, category, winner and film title. The table here shows examples of the data that is used by the Oscar app.

Year	Category	Winner	Film
1927	Best Actor	Emil Jannings	The Way of All Flesh
1927	Best Actress	Janet Gaynor	7th Heaven
1927	Best Picture	Wings	Wings
1927	Best Director	Frank Borzage	7th Heaven
1927	Best Original Story	Ben Hecht	Underworld

(a) Define a suitable data structure to hold the details of one Oscar winner.

(b) In total, there have been 2,947 Oscar winners.

Declare a suitable data structure that can be used to store the details of all the Oscar winners.

(c) The app requires a feature that will allow the user to enter the name of a film and then display the number of Oscars won by that film.

Using pseudocode, write an algorithm that will perform the required feature.

DON'T FORGET

The SQA reference language specifies the format to be used for record data structures in exam questions. You can either use the programming language that you use in your own school to implement record data structures, or learn the format of the SQA reference language to implement record data structures. The format of the SQA code is shown in this book in the "Implementation (structures)" spread.

THINGS TO DO AND THINK ABOUT

This course has an emphasis on problem-solving rather than memorising facts, but you still need to learn the theory covered in this book before you can apply it to solve problems.

Study the four standard algorithms (LINEAR SEARCH, FINDING MAXIMUM, FINDING MINIMUM, COUNTING OCCURRENCES), then take a piece of blank paper and try to write them out.

REVISION QUESTIONS 2

QUESTION 1

A program is used to enter and process the results of a cross-country running competition. The program enters the name, sex, year group, age and finishing time of each competitor.

The program stores the details for 80 competitors using different data types.

(a) (i) Explain the term "data type".

(ii) What data structure and data type would be used within the program to store the names of the 80 competitors?

(b) Four standard algorithms are:

1 linear search

2 counting occurrences

3 finding maximum

4 finding minimum.

Which standard algorithms would the program use to find:

(i) the number of girls in the race

(ii) the best time for the race?

(c) On the day of the race, the finishing times of the 80 competitors are entered into the program.

An athlete who runs the race in less than 12 minutes gains a star award.

Using a design notation with which you are familiar, write an algorithm which would find the number of athletes who gained a star award.

(d) The program was designed with a high level of modular independence.

(i) Explain how the use of local and global variables impacts on modular independence.

(ii) Describe one benefit of developing software with independent modules.

DON'T FORGET

When answering questions, it is important that your handwriting is reasonably neat. It does not need to be a work of art, but it is difficult to gain marks if the marker can't read your answer!

QUESTION 2

Testing of software can never show that the software is error-free, but it should be as comprehensive as possible given time and money constraints. Often, independent test groups are brought in to test the programs.

(a) Why do software-development companies employ independent test groups to test software, rather than let the software be tested by the programmers who wrote it?

(b) A program subroutine enters six test scores in the range 0...25 and calculates the number of fails (0...12), passes (13...22) and passes with distinction (23...25).

The subroutine should validate the scores in the range 0...25.

Give three sets of test data that could be used to test this subroutine fully, giving a reason why you have chosen each set of test data.

(Give the actual set of test-data values, and do not simply say "normal data" or "exceptional data".)

(c) For each set of test data, give the expected output from the subroutine.

QUESTION 3

A teacher uses a computer program in Geography. It stores a list of countries and their populations, from which the user can choose their own list of countries.

The program uses an algorithm to find the name of the country in the chosen list of countries with the highest population.

The list of chosen countries is stored in an array called CountryList, and the population of the chosen countries is stored in an array called PopulationList.

The code here is supposed to find the name of the country with the highest population and store it in a variable called MaxCountry.

```
LINE 1   SET MaxPopulation TO PopulationList[0]
LINE 2   FOR Index FROM 1 TO SizeofList – 1
LINE 3        IF PopulationList[Index] > MaxPopulation THEN
LINE 4            SET MaxCountry TO CountryList[Index]
LINE 5        END IF
LINE 6   END FOR
LINE 7   SEND [MaxCountry] TO DISPLAY
```

The code did not work properly when tested with the list of countries and populations shown below.

CountryList["Australia", "France", "Japan", "Italy", "Canada"]
PopulationList[32268240, 60495540, 128084700, 58092740, 20155130]

(a) Complete the last four rows of the trace table below, recording the value assigned to the variables.

(b) Explain why the code does not work properly by describing how the values stored in variables are updated as the program steps through the code.

Rewrite the complete algorithm so that it gives correct results.

	MaxPopulation	Index	MaxCountry
Line 1	32268240		
Line 2		1	
Line 4			France
Line 2		2	
Line 4			Japan
Line 2			
Line 4			
Line 2			
Line 4			

DON'T FORGET

It is a common mistake, when asked to supply sets of test data, just to say "normal, extreme and exceptional". You must give actual examples of test data that is to be entered into the program. In this question, you must give six actual numbers for each set of test data.

THINGS TO DO AND THINK ABOUT

Go to the SQA website and find the Higher Computing Science page. You will find that the "Resources" section has a "Course support" tab.

Open this tab and download the two PDF documents named "Reference language for Computing Science" and "Reference language for Computing Science (summary)".

The "Reference language for Computing Science" document contains lots of examples of code that you can study and use for revision.

The summary document gives a list of command words for programming features that can be used as a checklist that you know their format.

COMPUTER SYSTEMS

DATA REPRESENTATION (NUMBERS)

VIDEO LINK

Learn more about the binary number system by watching the clip at www.brightredbooks.net

WHOLE NUMBERS

Whole numbers include zero and positive numbers but not fractions, i.e. 0, 1, 2, 3, 4, 5, 6, 7 … These numbers are stored in a computer in binary, which is a number system based on powers of 2.

The example below shows how the number 45,685 is stored in 16-bit binary.

32768	16384	8192	4096	2048	1024	512	256	128	64	32	16	8	4	2	1
1	0	1	1	0	0	1	0	0	1	1	1	0	1	0	1

$32,768 + 8,192 + 4,096 + 512 + 64 + 32 + 16 + 4 + 1 = 45,685$

Conversion of Whole Numbers to Binary

The number is divided by two over and over again until zero is reached. The binary number is then obtained from the remainders. (Read the remainders from bottom to top.)

Example:

This example shows how to convert the number 41,800 into 16-bit binary:

```
2 | 41800
2 | 20900   R 0
2 | 10450   R 0
2 |  5225   R 0
2 |  2612   R 1
2 |  1306   R 0
2 |   653   R 0
2 |   326   R 1
2 |   163   R 0
2 |    81   R 1
2 |    40   R 1
2 |    20   R 0
2 |    10   R 0
2 |     5   R 0
2 |     2   R 1
2 |     1   R 0
2 |     0   R 1
```

Answer: 1010001101001000

DON'T FORGET

It is a common mistake to read the remainders from top to bottom. You must read the remainders from bottom to top.

DON'T FORGET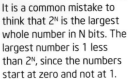

It is a common mistake to think that 2^N is the largest whole number in N bits. The largest number is 1 less than 2^N, since the numbers start at zero and not at 1.

For example, 16 bits can store 2^{16} numbers. This gives a range of numbers from 0 to $2^{16} - 1$ (0...65,535).

No. of bits	Numbers	No. of numbers
1	0, 1	2
2	00, 01, 10, 11	4
3	000, 001, 010, 011, 100, 101, 110, 111	8
...	...	...
8	...	256
N		2^N

RANGE OF NUMBERS

The number of different binary numbers that can be represented in a given number of bits is shown in the table.

Number of bits	8	16	24	32
Range of numbers	$0...2^8 - 1$	$0...2^{16} - 1$	$0...2^{24} - 1$	$0...2^{32} - 1$

INTEGERS

Computers use a system called two's complement to store integers. The most significant bit represents (–128), and the remaining bits are the same as for whole numbers.

The table below shows the range of numbers that can be represented in 8-bit two's complement.

contd

Example:

This example shows how the number (–83) is stored in 8-bit two's complement.

–128	64	32	16	8	4	2	1
1	0	1	0	1	1	0	1

–128 + 32 + 8 + 4 + 1 = (–83)

A larger range of numbers can be represented in two's complement by using 16 bits, 24 bits etc., with the most significant bit being a negative value.

	–128	64	32	16	8	4	2	1	
Largest	0	1	1	1	1	1	1	1	127
Smallest	1	0	0	0	0	0	0	0	–128

ONLINE

Have a look at floating-point numbers in the YouTube video www.youtube.com/watch?v=KkFLnnneZ2k, which gives a graphical description of the component parts of a floating-point number.

REAL NUMBERS

Computers use a system called floating point to store real numbers. The floating-point number is made up of the mantissa, which holds the significant figures of the number, and the exponent, which holds the power.

An advantage of floating-point notation is that very large and very small numbers can be stored in a small number of bits.

Example:

$$\boxed{\text{Mantissa}} \rightarrow 0\cdot10110011 \times 2^{11101001} \leftarrow \boxed{\text{Exponent}}$$

A disadvantage of floating-point notation is that precision is lost, since the mantissa only gives the number to a certain amount of significant figures.

Range and Precision of Floating-Point Numbers

Increasing the number of bits assigned to the **exponent** increases the **range** of numbers.

Increasing the number of bits assigned to the **mantissa** increases the **precision** of the number.

Positive and Negative

A sign bit is used in the mantissa to represent a positive number with a 0 and a negative number with a 1. The exponent is represented in two's complement, giving a range from –128 to 127 for an 8-bit exponent.

The table below illustrates some examples of positive, negative, large and small floating-point numbers using a 15-bit mantissa and an 8-bit exponent.

Number	Sign bit	Mantissa (15-bit)	Exponent (8-bit)	Floating point
Large +ve	0	100001010100000	01111111	$0\cdot1000010101 \times 2^{01111111}$
Large –ve	1	101000110000000	01111111	$-0\cdot10100011 \times 2^{01111111}$
Small +ve	0	101010000000000	10000000	$0\cdot10101 \times 2^{10000000}$
Small –ve	1	110100000000000	10000000	$-0\cdot1101 \times 2^{10000000}$

ONLINE

Use a search engine to investigate the difference in the representation of single and double data types in the Visual Basic programming language.

VIDEO LINK

Learn more about floating-point numbers by watching the clip at www.brightredbooks.net

ONLINE TEST

Take the test on Data Representation (numbers) at www.brightredbooks.net

 THINGS TO DO AND THINK ABOUT

Go online and research how Visual Basic and Python use bytes to represent integers and real numbers.

Find out how many bytes each language uses to store a two's complement number and a floating-point number and how the bytes are allocated to the number.

DATA REPRESENTATION (TEXT AND GRAPHICS)

INTRODUCTION

Text and graphics appear widely in newspapers, glossy magazines, catalogues, websites and so on.

Text can be stored in English or in other world languages, and standards have been developed for doing this in a computer system.

There are two types of graphics program – called bit-mapped graphics and vector graphics. Each of these programs stores and edits an image in different ways.

Each has different advantages over the other, and the choice of which type of graphic to use depends on the image that is being created or edited.

TEXT

Text in a computer system is represented by using a binary code for each character.

Extended ASCII and Unicode are two standards that have been developed for text representation.

The extended ASCII system is based on the English alphabet and represents each character in 8 bits. This system allows for 28 = 256 different codes. This is sufficient to represent the 26 uppercase and 26 lowercase letters, a few dozen punctuation characters, the symbols for the digits 0, 1, 2, 3...9, and control characters that are all found in the English language.

The ASCII code language is limited in that it can only store 256 characters. This is fine for the English alphabet but does not cater for characters in foreign languages throughout the world such as Japanese, Arabic and so on.

The Unicode system is a solution to this problem in that it uses 16 bits to encode each character, allowing for 216 = 65,536 codes.

Comparison of Extended ASCII and Unicode

- Extended ASCII has fewer storage requirements than Unicode, since it uses 1 byte to store each character, whereas Unicode uses 2 bytes.

- Unicode can store 65,536 characters, whereas ASCII can only store 256 characters.

BIT-MAPPED GRAPHICS

This type of graphics stores an image as colour codes for a two-dimensional grid of pixels. The term "pixel" comes from "picture element" and is the dots that make up the graphic.

Bit-mapped graphics programs will have tools such as a rubber and a paint spraycan so that the colour of individual pixels can be changed.

Bit Depth

The bit depth is the number of bits that are used as the code for the colour of each pixel.

The simplest bit depth is 1 bit, which can encode two colours (usually black and white), since 1 bit has two codes (1 and 0), which can be used to represent both colours.

An image using 8-bit depth will be able to represent 2^8 = 256 colours.

An image using 16-bit depth will be able to represent 2^{16} = 65,536 colours.

contd

An image using 24-bit depth will be able to represent $2^{24} = 16,777,216$ colours.

A bit depth of 24 bits is called true colour, since it represents the limit of the number of colours that the human eye can recognise. This is a commonly used bit depth for bit-mapped graphics programs.

Resolution

The resolution is the size of the pixels and is usually measured in dots per inch (dpi).

High-resolution graphics are made up of a large number of small pixels.

Low-resolution graphics are made up of a small number of large pixels.

Resolution is a factor that will affect the quality of an image. High-resolution graphics will have more detail than low-resolution graphics and will consequently produce a more accurate image. The drawback is that high-resolution graphics have larger storage requirements.

VECTOR GRAPHICS

This type of graphics stores an image as a list of objects, each of which is described by its attributes. The attributes are features that describe an object, such as its starting coordinates, length, fill colour, line thickness and so on.

Low resolution

High resolution

For example, the image shown here consists of Rectangle, Circle and Textbox objects.

Each object is stored by its attributes:

Example:

Rectangle: start x, start y, length, breadth, fill colour, line colour, line thickness, line pattern etc.
Circle: centre x, centre y, radius, fill colour, line colour, line thickness etc.
Textbox: start x, start y, text, font, fontsize, fill colour, line colour, line thickness, etc.

Large and Small Size Clothes

Bit-mapped Graphics vs Vector Graphics

- Bit-mapped graphics in general have a larger storage requirement than vector graphics, since the colour codes for thousands or millions of pixels have to be stored.

- Vector graphics only need to store codes for the objects and attributes that the image is composed of.

- A bit-mapped image will become pixellated and jagged when enlarged, since the resolution is fixed for the original image.

- A vector graphic will not become pixellated, since the resolution is not fixed and the objects' attributes are simply changed to match the enlarged objects.

- Parts of a bit-mapped graphic cannot be separated without leaving blank areas of pixels, but in vector graphics overlapping objects can be separated or layered in different orders.

- Bit-mapped graphics can be edited in fine detail by editing individual pixels, but vector graphics are edited by changing the attributes of an object such as the fill colour, line thickness etc.

THINGS TO DO AND THINK ABOUT

Try to create a chessboard using first a bit-mapped graphics program such as Microsoft Paint and then with vector graphics such as the Drawing tools in Microsoft Word. Compare how easy it is to perform this task in the two packages, and consider why it is easier in one package than the other.

COMPUTER STRUCTURE

FETCH-EXECUTE CYCLE

A computer solves a problem by storing a set of instructions (a program) in memory that are then fetched and executed one at a time to solve a problem. This is called the "stored program concept".

Processor Buses

The CPU has buses, which are multiple wires/lines that connect the processor and main memory. They are used to carry data, to specify memory-location addresses, and to send signals between them.

Data Bus

This bus is used to transfer data between main memory and the processor. It is a two-way bus, since data can be transferred from a memory location to the processor and vice versa.

Early computers had a data bus that was 8 lines wide and transferred 8 bits in a single operation. Modern desktop computers will typically have a 64-bit data bus.

The number of bits that the processor transfers in one operation is called the word size.

Address Bus

This bus is used to specify the address of the memory location that is to be read from or written to. This bus is a one-way bus, since the processor will use it to specify which memory location it is going to use; but the reverse does not apply.

Early computers had an address bus that was 16 lines wide. Modern desktop computers will typically have a 32-bit address bus.

Control Bus

Each of the control-bus lines has a specific function. Here are the functions of some control-bus lines:

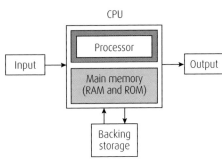

CPU

- Read – A signal down this line is used to initiate a memory READ operation, which reads the contents of a memory location into the processor.

- Write – A signal down this line is used to initiate a memory WRITE operation, which writes an item of data from the processor into a memory location.

- Clock – The clock line sends a regular series of pulses into the processor to synchronise events. The time interval between each pulse is called a clock cycle. For example, a memory read or a memory write takes place in one clock cycle.

- Reset – A signal down this line causes the computer to stop execution of the current program and then to reboot.

Memory Read and Write Operations

Memory READ

A processor reads instructions from memory as part of the fetch–execute cycle.

Step 1   The processor sets up the address bus with the address of the required memory location.
Step 2   The processor activates the READ line on the control bus.
Step 3   The contents of the memory location are transferred along the data bus into the processor.

contd

Step 4   The instruction is decoded and executed.

Memory WRITE

Step 1   The processor sets up the address bus with the address of the required memory location.

Step 2   The processor sets up the data bus with the data to be written to memory.

Step 3   The processor activates the WRITE line on the control bus.

Step 4   The data is transferred along the data bus to the memory location.

FACTORS AFFECTING SYSTEM PERFORMANCE

The performance of computers has improved considerably over the last few decades as the technology advances. There are several factors that have contributed to this improvement.

Number of Processors (cores)

Processors were originally developed with only one core, which meant that they could only execute one instruction at any given instant. In recent years, there has been a move towards multi-core processors, i.e. a single chip with two or more processor components (called cores) which can independently execute program instructions.

Multi-core processors can execute multiple instructions at the same time, thus increasing the overall speed of program execution.

Width of Data Bus

Increasing the width of the data bus improves system performance, since more bits are transferred between the processor and memory in a read or write operation. The data-bus width in desktop computers has increased from typically 8 bits in early computers to typically 32 bits in a current desktop/laptop computer.

Cache Memory

This is an area of fast-access memory either between the processor and main memory or on the processor chip itself. The cache holds instructions and data that are used most frequently. Since these are in fast-access storage, it increases the overall performance of the system.

Clock Speed

Every processor uses a clock which sends a regular series of pulses into the processor to synchronise events. The time interval between each pulse is called a clock cycle. For example, a memory read or a memory write takes place in one clock cycle.

Increasing the clock speed means that more memory read/writes happen per second and so increases the amount of data being processed per second.

A typical clock speed of 4 GHz performs four billion cycles a second.

THINGS TO DO AND THINK ABOUT

Computing hardware is constantly developing in performance, and new technologies are constantly appearing. You should read computing magazines and visit websites (PC World, Dell etc.) to get a feel for the current specification of devices. This will widen your understanding and will allow you to bring more depth to your answers.

DON'T FORGET

There are many factors that improve system performance. The factors required for this course are multi-core processors, increasing the width of the data bus, cache memory and increasing the clock speed of the processor.

ONLINE

Learn more about computer cache at www.computer. howstuffworks.com/ cache.htm, which gives a description, advantages and deeper technical detail of how computer cache works.

VIDEO LINK

Learn more about computer architecture by watching the clip at www.brightredbooks.net

VIDEO LINK

Learn more about computer cache by watching the clip at www.brightredbooks.net

ONLINE TEST

Take the test on Computer Structure at www.brightredbooks.net

ENVIRONMENTAL IMPACT OF INTELLIGENT SYSTEMS

INTELLIGENT SYSTEMS

Intelligent systems are computer systems that use Artificial Intelligence to imitate human intelligence. They are used to perform tasks that would normally require humans, such as autopilots for flying planes, credit-card fraud protection, robotic vacuum cleaners etc.

Increasing processing power and improving AI techniques such as image recognition, touch-sensing and speech recognition are producing new levels of functionality for tasks that until recently were only performed by humans.

Autonomous unmanned vehicles have sensors and AI software that allow them to act independently rather than being remotely controlled by a human operator. Intelligent robots are able to work in environments that are dangerous for humans, such as deep-sea exploration, outer space and war zones. There are enormous ethical questions to be answered about the use of vehicles that act independently as a weapon of war.

This course specifies three areas of the use of intelligent systems and their environmental impact:

1   Heating systems

2   Traffic-control systems

3   Car-management systems.

Environmental impact

Human activity can have a negative environmental impact through the release of greenhouse gases by burning fossil fuels. Intelligent systems can help to reduce this impact by providing systems that are more efficient in their energy requirements and lead to a reduced fuel consumption and lower emissions.

For example, an intelligent system that is used to plan the distribution of goods by lorries can find routes that minimise the overall journey distance and reduce the environmental impact.

DON'T FORGET

For this course, you must know the environmental impact of intelligent systems that are for heating, traffic control and car management. You do not need to know about the impact of other intelligent systems such as robotics and fraud detection.

HEATING SYSTEMS

Early central-heating systems used thermostats that could be set manually to control the heat emitted by individual radiators and offer some control over the efficiency of the system.

Modern heating systems offer more efficient control by intelligently adapting to the day-to-day use of the system. For example, the heating system can learn from previous data what temperatures are preferred in which rooms and at what time of day.

Movement sensors can be fitted in each room which can monitor the amount of activity in each room and increase or reduce the heat accordingly. If nobody has gone into a spare room for three days, then the heating can be switched off in that room until activity resumes.

Smartphones can connect via wi-fi and use an app that allows the heat in each room to be adjusted from the phone and can turn the heating on from a remote location to heat the house in time for returning home.

TRAFFIC-CONTROL SYSTEMS

The speed of traffic has a big impact on the fuel consumption of vehicles, since free-flowing traffic which is moving between 50 and 60 miles per hour has a much lower fuel consumption than traffic that is starting and stopping because of congestion on busy roads.

Intelligent traffic-control systems use data from sensors and cameras to intelligently control traffic signals to optimise the traffic flow and thereby limit fuel consumption.

Satnav systems can also be used to guide drivers through less congested routes and improve the overall flow of traffic.

In the future, self-driving cars will monitor traffic, weather and road conditions to always take the most efficient (in terms of energy) route to the destination.

CAR-MANAGEMENT SYSTEMS

Car-management systems are ways of reducing the fuel consumption of cars and lorries and other vehicles by intelligently managing the vehicle's engine through computer control.

For example, the engine can be made to automatically turn off when the car is stopped at traffic lights and to automatically restart when the driver accelerates to move off.

In town, a lot of time is spent stopping and starting at traffic lights, and the fuel that is consumed by cars whose engine is idling when stopped at traffic lights and in traffic jams can be reduced.

Sensors can also be used to optimise engine performance by controlling the air-to-fuel ratio accurately for the best fuel consumption.

In the future, electric cars aim to get as many miles out of the battery as possible to reduce the number of times it needs to be charged and hence reduce the emissions from power stations.

THINGS TO DO AND THINK ABOUT

Intelligent systems have a positive and/or negative impact on the environment, economy and society.

Office buildings are increasingly using robotic vacuum cleaners to clean the rooms after working hours. List the impact on the environment, economy and society of using robots to do this work instead of humans.

Also, consider if there is any negative environmental impact of using robotic vacuum cleaners. Try to list at least two negative impacts.

DON'T FORGET

Intelligent traffic-control systems are about having an efficient flow of traffic to reduce fuel consumption, whereas intelligent car-management systems are about efficient fuel consumption by the vehicle's engine.

ONLINE

Visit YouTube and watch a short video on intelligent heating systems at www.youtube.com/watch?v=tlnC6E8p7R8&t=28s

ONLINE TEST

Take the test on Environmental Impact of Intelligent Systems at www.brightredbooks.net

SECURITY RISKS AND PRECAUTIONS

THE COMPUTER MISUSE ACT 1990

This act is concerned with the misuse of computing technology to hack into confidential data and to purposely send destructive viruses to other people's computers.

Hacking into computer systems has been around as long as the internet.

One of the problems with global communication is that it can be misused to gain access to confidential information to view it, change it or delete it. Before this act was introduced, there was no specific law that made these activities illegal.

The following activities are made illegal by the Computer Misuse Act:

- Gaining access to data held on a computer without permission, e.g. looking at someone else's files

- Gaining access to data held on a computer with the intention to commit a criminal offence, e.g. hacking into a bank's computer and trying to increase the amount in your account

- Altering data held on a computer without permission, e.g. writing a virus to destroy someone else's data.

TRACKING COOKIES

A cookie stores data on a user's computer to remember the user's activities when visiting a website.

For example, cookies can store a username and password so that you do not have to sign in every time you return to a website. A cookie can also track your preferences and show you other websites that might be of interest to you.

Some of the benefits of cookies are also seen as negative. For example, one of the most common ways of online theft is by hackers taking confidential information such as usernames and passwords that a cookie saves.

The browsing habits and frequently visited websites which are saved in cookies can be sold to other companies, who can then flood the user with unwanted junk e-mail.

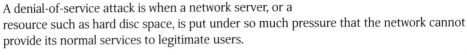

DoS (DENIAL-OF-SERVICE) ATTACK

A denial-of-service attack is when a network server, or a resource such as hard disc space, is put under so much pressure that the network cannot provide its normal services to legitimate users.

DoS attacks involve bombarding the network with a high volume of data in a short period of time so that the network cannot cope.

Symptoms of an Attack

The symptoms of a DoS attack are that the performance of the system becomes slow or grinds to a halt and prevents users from accessing the system.

contd

Types of Attack

Bandwidth consumption

This attack degrades the performance of a server by sending it a large number of data packets in a short period of time. For example, a smurf attack is mounted by sending a packet with a false source address to the broadcast address of a network. (Giving a packet a false source address is called spoofing.) The packet contains a ping message, which is a technique for checking that a communication link is working properly.

All of the computers on the network then reply to the ping message, which is actually the address of the target server.

Resource starvation

An attack can consume other resources apart from bandwidth in order to bring down a server.

For example, the server's hard-disc space can be used up by sending a large volume of e-mail messages.

Domain Name Service (DNS)

In this attack, a large number of DNS queries with a spoofed IP address of the target server are sent to a DNS server. The DNS server then floods the target server with an excessive number of replies.

Reasons for Attacks

There are several reasons why DoS attacks are carried out.

Malicious
Individuals think that it is good fun to bring down an organisation's network.

Personal
Disgruntled employees who bear a grudge can see a DoS attack as revenge against their employer.

Political
Sometimes, DoS attacks can be politically motivated, such as an attack on a government network, or to bring down a rival company in business.

Costs of Attacks

A DoS attack can be very costly to an organisation – for several reasons:

1   The loss of business during the attack downtime

2   The cost of repair and response to the attack

3   Users' loss of confidence in the organisation.

 **DON'T FORGET**

It is a common mistake to state that a DoS attack is brought about by flooding a server with a vast amount of data but not mentioning that it is in a short period of time. It is the fact that the server can't deal with a large volume of data in a short period of time that brings it down.

 ONLINE

Learn more about denial-of-service attacks by watching the YouTube video at www.youtube.com/watch?v=c9EjuOQRUdg

 THINGS TO DO AND THINK ABOUT

There have been many famous DoS attacks, ranging from political attacks on government networks to "fun" attacks carried out by teenage boys.

Use the internet to investigate famous DoS attacks.

Who committed each attack, what was the motivation for the attack, and what was the impact of the attack for the victim?

 ONLINE TEST

Take the test on Security Risks and Precautions at www.brightredbooks.net

ENCRYPTION

INTRODUCTION

Encryption takes place in many situations where data is being transmitted over an internet connection. Examples are personal banking apps, online payment methods and messaging apps.

Encryption is the process of encoding data, making it unintelligible and scrambled. In most cases, the encrypted data is paired with an encryption key, and the encrypted data can only be opened by someone who possesses the key.

An encryption key is a collection of algorithms designed to be totally unique. These are able to scramble and unscramble data, essentially unlocking the information and turning it back to readable data.

Usually, the person who is encrypting the data will possess the key that locks the data, and will make "copies" and pass them on to relevant people who require access. This process is called public-key cryptography.

Encryption became significant during the Second World War, with military forces across Europe tasked with breaking Nazi Germany's Enigma code.

SYMMETRIC ENCRYPTION

Symmetric encryption is the simplest form of encryption. It encrypts data using a secret key and an encryption algorithm. Both the sender and the receiver need to have a copy of the secret key, which is kept secure.

The encryption algorithm processes the data with the secret key to produce ciphertext, which is transmitted over the insecure channel.

The receiver applies the secret key to the ciphertext using the decryption algorithm in order to retrieve the original data.

Symmetric encryption is simple and fast to implement, but it is difficult to manage the exchange of the secret key over an insecure channel.

ASYMMETRIC ENCRYPTION

Public and Private Keys

Asymmetric encryption is a more complex encryption method that uses a combination of a public and a private key to encrypt data.

If the public key is used to encrypt the message, then only the private key can be used with the decryption algorithm in order to retrieve the original data.

If the private key is used for encryption, then the resulting ciphertext can only be decrypted using that person's public key to ensure that the message is from who it claims to be from.

Asymmetric encryption is more complicated and slower to implement than symmetric encryption but is much more secure.

One of the benefits of asymmetric encryption is that the sender and the receiver do not need to exchange a private key first. The public key is available to anyone who needs to send an encrypted message to the receiver, but only the receiver can decrypt it because only the receiver has the private key.

contd

Digital Certificates

A digital certificate is a package of information that identifies a user with information such as the user's name, the name of the organisation that issued the certificate (the Certificate Authority), the user's e-mail address and country, and the user's public key.

The certificate authority acts as a middleman that both users trust. It confirms the identity of each user and provides the public keys of each user to the other.

When two users require a secure encrypted communication, one sends a query over the internet to the other user, who sends back a copy of the certificate.

The other user's public key can be extracted from the certificate.

Digital Signatures

A digital signature is a piece of code that can be attached to a message which uniquely identifies the sender and therefore guarantees that the message is from the person it claims to be from. A digital signature can also be used to ensure that the message has not been altered.

The public and private key system can be used to create digital signatures. The private key can be used to attach a digital signature to data being transmitted. A hashing algorithm is applied to the data to be transmitted to create a unique message digest.

This message digest is encrypted using the private key and is transmitted along with the data as a digital signature.

At the receiving end, the hashing algorithm is applied to the message to produce the message digest, and the attached signature is decrypted using the sender's public key to produce the original message digest. If the two message digests are identical, then the recipient knows that the signature is valid and that the data has not been tampered with in transit.

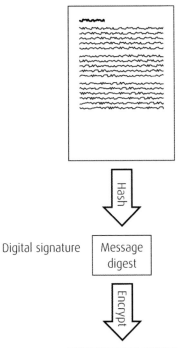

Digital signature → Hash → Message digest → Encrypt → Signature

DON'T FORGET

In asymmetric encryption, the public and private keys work as a pair. If the private key is used to encrypt the data, then only the paired public key can decrypt the data. If the public key is used to encrypt the data, then only the paired private key can decrypt the data.

ONLINE

Find out more about digital signatures on the website www.youdzone.com/signature.html

VIDEO LINK

Learn more about digital signatures by watching the clip at www.brightredbooks.net

ONLINE TEST

Take the test on Encryption at www.brightredbooks.net

THINGS TO DO AND THINK ABOUT

Think about where encryption is used in the apps and websites that you use. Is the sensitive data on your phone encrypted?

Also, investigate the sort of encryption that is used on your school network. Ask your network manager how encryption is used to protect data on the school network and the technical details underlying the technology.

Try to find out if all files are encrypted or only sensitive files such as passwords and staff salary information.

REVISION QUESTIONS 1

QUESTION 1

Standards have been developed for representing numbers, text and graphics in binary in computer systems.

73 JFK

(a) Why do standards exist for the storage of data on computer systems?

(b) What is the largest **whole number** that can be stored as a 32-bit positive integer?

(c) What is the largest positive integer that can be stored in 16-bit two's complement?

(d) A programmer is writing a program to process results of the 100 metres event at the Olympic Games.

The program needs to store the athletes' times to 2 decimal places.

The programmer is using a language that has two floating-point data types, called "Real" and "Surreal". "Real" has an 8-bit mantissa and an 8-bit exponent. "Surreal" has a 24-bit mantissa and a 16-bit exponent.

State whether the "Real" or the "Surreal" data type is better suited for storing the athletes' times, and justify your answer.

(e) Unicode and Extended ASCII are standards for representing text in a computer system.

Give one advantage that each standard has over the other.

(f) The image of the logo shown here was created using a vector graphics package.

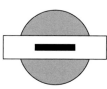

Explain how the image shown would be stored in vector graphics.

QUESTION 2

A catalogue is to be produced for a mail-order company that makes garden gnomes. The catalogue will have 80 pages which will contain photographs and descriptions of gnomes. Each of the images will measure 2 × 1·5 inches and will be created in a bit-mapped package in 16-bit colour and 100 dpi.

(a) The resolution of the images is planned to be 100 dpi.

(i) Why is this not a suitable resolution for the images in this situation?

(ii) Suggest a more suitable resolution, and describe any disadvantage of changing to this resolution.

(b) Suggest why a vector graphics package is not suitable for creating the gnome images, and justify your answer.

(c) A sample of the photographs has to be sent to the company director as e-mail attachments so that he can approve them.

contd

Name a standard file format that could be used for these graphics files.

(d) The director is not pleased with the quality of the photographs, and asks for the photographs to be retaken in true colour.

What effect would this have on the storage requirements for the photographs?

QUESTION 3

This diagram shows the simplified structure of a computer system.

C, A and D represent the three processor buses.

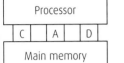

C = Control bus
A = Address bus (32 bits)
D = Data bus (32 bits)

(a) Describe the steps involved when the processor fetches and executes an instruction held in main memory.

(Your answer should refer to the roles of processor buses and registers.)

(b) (i) Explain how the control bus differs from the address and data bus.

(ii) State the name of two lines on the control bus, and describe each of their functions.

(c) (i) Modern processors use cache to improve their performance.

Explain how cache improves processor performance.

(ii) Cache is only one of several ways of improving the performance of a processor.

Describe another way of improving the performance of a processor.

THINGS TO DO AND THINK ABOUT

The content of this course changed significantly for the school year starting in August 2018. This means that exam papers before this year do not adequately cover the current course. These old exam papers are still useful for revision. The SQA have published a document which shows you which questions from old exam papers are still useful. You should be able to obtain this document from your teacher, or find it at www.brightredbooks.net

You may also find, when doing revision questions from different resources, that you feel that you have not covered the work required for a question. It may well be that the material is based on the content for the old course – so make sure that you ask your teacher for guidance in this situation.

You can use the Syllabus and Assessment spread at the start of this book as a check for the course content, but make sure that you ask your teacher if you are unsure.

REVISION QUESTIONS 2

QUESTION 1

Some numbers are whole numbers, such as the number of people on a bus or the number of puppies in a litter. Other numbers are decimal fractions, such as the average daily temperature in Edinburgh in July or the weight of a rhinoceros in kilograms.

(a) Computer systems store numbers in two's complement and floating-point notation.

Describe the difference between the two types of numbers that these two systems represent.

(b) Convert the following numbers to 8-bit two's complement:

(i) 81

(ii) −25

(c) Convert the following 16-bit binary number to decimal:

0010000101111011

(d) Convert the following decimal number to 16-bit binary:

34,645

DON'T FORGET

Two's complement and floating-point notations are both used to represent numbers in a computer system. You should know how each system represents the number and be able to convert decimal numbers into binary and binary numbers into decimal.

QUESTION 2

Money World is an online currency exchange company that buys and sells worldwide currencies.

(a) Customers of Money World can register an account to buy a currency, sell a currency and update their contact details when required.

(i) Explain how the customers' details and transactions can be kept secure when they are transmitted.

(ii) When Money World began their business, they applied for a digital certificate.

Give two items of data that are included in a digital certificate.

(iii) From time to time, customers receive messages from Money World requesting confidential information.

How can the customer be sure that the message has come from Money World and that they are not a victim of a fraudulent activity?

(b) Money World have a team of motorbike riders that they use for the deliveries of currency orders. The motorbike riders make use of an intelligent traffic-control system.

(i) Describe **two** ways in which an intelligent traffic-control system can have a positive impact on the environment.

(ii) Describe **one** negative impact on the environment of an intelligent traffic-control system.

DON'T FORGET

This course covers several intelligent systems that include heating systems, traffic-control systems and car-management systems. You are required to know about the environmental impact of these systems but not their economic or social impact.

QUESTION 3

Resolution College of Photography is a training college for graphic designers and students of photography.

Its computers are linked together in a computer network, with applications and data files held on the network server. The network is used by teachers, students and administrators, and users can access their network data remotely so that they can work from home.

(a) Last session, a member of staff gained access to confidential data held on the college network and added £1,000 to their salary.

Which law makes this sort of activity illegal?

(b) Some of the students in the college are concerned that they can't change the browser settings on their computers to block tracking cookies.

(i) What is a tracking cookie?

(ii) Why might the students be concerned about tracking cookies?

(c) Recently, Remount College was the victim of a DOS attack which seriously reduced the performance of the network to a point that it was extremely slow and unusable by the teachers and students.

(i) Expand the acronym DOS.

(ii) Describe a type of DOS attack that could prevent access to legitimate users of the college network.

(iii) Describe two possible costs to the college of this attack.

(iv) Suggest a reason why a DOS attack would be carried out by a company or an individual.

 DON'T FORGET

Remember that this course is not entirely about technical issues. You are also expected to have knowledge of wider issues such as those in the spread on the "Environmental Impact of Intelligent Systems".

 DON'T FORGET

The *Things to do and think about* mention using precise language in your answers. For example, to describe vector graphics as representing an image as a bunch of shapes with different features gives some indication of how vector graphics work but does not use the appropriate terminology. A much better answer would be to describe vector graphics as representing an image as a list of objects such as rectangles, circles etc. and their attributes such as centre x, centre y, radius, fill colour, line colour, line thickness etc.

 THINGS TO DO AND THINK ABOUT

Students often do not finish an exam in time, or rush to complete the last questions and often end up not answering them fully.

You need to find a balance between giving full and detailed answers and writing answers that are too lengthy and put you under pressure to complete the exam. Don't be too vague with the language you use in your answers. Make sure that you use any relevant technical terms and explain/describe with precise and detailed sentences – see an example in the *Don't forget* to the right.

If you have additional support for learning arrangements, then make sure that you know what form this will take.

Find out exactly how much extra time you will be given in the exam, or if you are to use a laptop or perhaps have a reader/scribe. All of these factors will have an impact on your speed of working during the exam.

ANALYSIS

INTRODUCTION

The first stage when developing a database to solve a problem is to analyse what the user wants the program to do.

Meetings are held between the developers of the database system and the end users to determine what they require from the software. It is important to identify the types of user that will use the system and what data they will need to enter, process and output. Existing manual documents can be studied to gain an understanding of the current manual system and to look for improvements that can be incorporated into the computerised database.

END-USER AND FUNCTIONAL REQUIREMENTS

End-user requirements

When a database is being developed, the type of users that are going to use the system and their requirements must be considered.

The end users are the people who are actually going to use the database, and it is essential to identify the tasks that they expect to be able to do using the database.

There are two main considerations:

1   the age range of the end users

2   the experience level of the end users.

The age range is important, since young children should be given an interface with big pictures, bright colours, and large buttons to click on, with not too much text which would be confusing to young children and reduce the usability of the software. If the database is to be used by adults, then the interface can contain more text and small icons and buttons that are easy for an adult to navigate.

A **novice** user is one who has little experience with database systems and requires an interface to suit their skill level. An **expert** user is one who is very familiar with database systems and is likely to be familiar with all the common features of database software. A database that is to be used by novice users might have a user interface which uses the mouse to make selections. If the database is intended for expert users, then it might be appropriate to use keyboard shortcuts to select the features they require.

Functional Requirements

The functional requirements state what functions the database software must carry out in order to meet the user requirements.

The functional requirements of a database will include functions such as validation of table data, queries, sorting, calculations, aggregate functions etc.

DON'T FORGET

The user requirements specify what tasks the end users expect to be able to do using the database from a human point of view. The functional requirements specify the information that the system has to contain and the processes the system has to perform to be able to carry out its functions.

EXAMPLE

The manager of a cat-grooming business requires a computer system to record and manage the grooming appointments.

The business has a list of cat owners, their cats and cat groomers. Grooming appointments are booked using a booking form.

contd

The manager wishes to be able to book appointments and view the appointments by owner, day or week. He also wants the system to automatically send e-mail reminders to the cat owners three days before their appointment date to avoid missed appointments and loss of business.

The system should calculate total monthly bills and generate invoices that can be e-mailed to the owners. The database should also calculate the total amount of money spent by each owner in the last six months so that they can be targeted for future promotions.

End-user requirements

The end-user requirements for the cat-grooming business are the tasks that the manager and staff expect to be able to carry out, such as:

- Enter details on cats, owners, cat groomers and bookings
- Search for appointments to answer telephone enquiries
- Display and print lists of daily and weekly bookings
- Send out appointment reminders automatically
- Prepare invoices for owners that show the full details of their booking.

Functional Requirements

The functional requirements of the database describe what input, processing and output the system must perform from a computing point of view as opposed to the end user's point of view.

This will include a description of the tables and their fields.

The cat-grooming database requires four tables: Cats, Owners, Groomers and Bookings.

Each table will require a primary key field, and foreign keys will be used to link the four tables together.

The database requires the four table and fields shown below:

CAT TABLE	OWNER TABLE	GROOMER TABLE	BOOKINGS TABLE
Cat_id	Owner_id	Groomer_id	Booking_id
Name	First name	First name	Date
Sex	Surname	Surname	Time
Breed	Address	Address	Cost
Age	Town	Town	Cat
Owner	Postcode	Postcode	Owner
	Telephone	Telephone	Groomer

The database requires the following functions:

- input validation of data entered into the Cat, Owner, Groomers and Bookings tables
- search queries to find booking appointments
- a query using today's date to create reminders of coming appointments
- a calculation to work out the total monthly bills for grooming appointments
- an aggregate function to calculate the total amount of money spent by each owner in the last six months.

ONLINE

The BBC Bitesize website has more information on database development and questions to assess your understanding.

DON'T FORGET

An essential part of the analysis stage of database development is to identify the tables that are required to store the information and the fields that are required in each table.

ONLINE TEST

Take the test on Analysis at www.brightredbooks.net

THINGS TO DO AND THINK ABOUT

A database must be accessible to suit the user requirements of all users, which includes those with vision, hearing and motor disabilities. Think about how accessible the databases are that you have created and how they could be improved. Choose one of your databases, and include accessibility features for people with hearing or vision problems.

DESIGN 1

INTRODUCTION

A relational database stores data in two or more linked tables. The main advantages of relating tables are improved accuracy and less duplication of data, since data is entered only once, and fewer errors result.

DATABASE DESIGN

An entity-relationship diagram is a method of design used to describe the entities and their attributes and the types of relationships between the entities in a relational database.

Database terminology uses the terms "entity" and "attribute" to refer to the tables and fields in a relational database respectively.

Entity

A relational database is composed of entities which can be a person, city, lesson, film etc. about which data is to be stored. For example, a Sports Day database might have entities such as Athlete, Judge, Event and Scorer.

Entity Occurrence

An actual example of an entity is called an instance of an entity, or an entity occurrence. For example, Zoe Hogg, Alex Foot and Sarah Davidson might be entity occurrences of the Athlete entity. High Jump, 400m and Javelin might be entity occurrences of the Event entity.

Attribute

Each entity has its own characteristics, which are described by its attributes. For example, the Athlete entity might have attributes such as athleteID, surname, age, gender etc.

Primary key

A primary key is an attribute that uniquely identifies one, and only one, occurrence of an entity. Underlining the attribute is used to indicate a primary key in an entity-relationship diagram.

Sometimes two or more attributes are used to indicate the primary key, which is called a compound key.

Foreign key

A foreign key is an attribute in one table that is used to uniquely identify a row in another table. An asterisk is used to indicate a foreign key in an entity-relationship diagram.

Relationship

The relationship is the way in which the entities are associated. For example, Athletes enter Events, Coaches teach Golfers, Agents manage Actors etc.

Cardinality

The cardinality of a relationship defines the number of entity occurrences in one entity that are associated with one occurrence of the related entity.

Cardinality can be:

- one-to-one
- one-to-many
- many-to-many.

ENTITY-RELATIONSHIP DIAGRAM

An entity-relationship diagram indicates:

- the name of each entity in the system
- the name of the relationship between two entities
- the cardinality of the relationship between two entities.
- Sometimes the name of each attribute can be shown.

Labelled rectangles are used to represent the entities in an entity-relationship diagram.

Sometimes the attributes of each entity are included, which are illustrated by labelled ovals. A line is drawn between two entities to join them, which is labelled with the name of the relationship. A crow's-foot notation is used to indicate the "many" sides of a relationship.

EXAMPLE

A relational database stores data on the Seven Dwarfs and orders that they place for items that they buy for their work in the diamond mines.

The table below shows the three entities required for the database and the attributes describing each entity.

The primary key in each entity is underlined, and foreign keys are followed by an asterisk.

Entity: Dwarf	Entity: Product	Entity: Order
dwarfID	productID	orderID
dwarfname	article	date
age	cost	dwarfID*
street	quantity	productID*
town	supplier	
postcode		
married		

ONE-TO-ONE RELATIONSHIP

The Dwarf entity is used to illustrate a one-to-one relationship between entities. A one-to-one relationship can sometimes be used to split a large entity into two smaller entities. In this example, the Dwarf entity is split into a Dwarf entity and an Address entity, with the two tables linked with the dwarfID foreign key.

Entity: Dwarf	Entity: Address
dwarfID	addressID
dwarfname	street
age	town
	postcode
	married
	dwarfID*

The term **one-to-one** refers to the fact that one occurrence in the Dwarf entity is linked to one, and only one, occurrence in the Address entity.

The one-to-one relationship is illustrated in the entity-relationship diagram shown here. This diagram represents the relationship between the Dwarf and Address entities.

💭 THINGS TO DO AND THINK ABOUT

A table that includes information on cars may have a RegistrationNumber field which can be used as the primary key. This type of key is called a **natural** key. A **surrogate** key is a new field with artificially generated values whose sole purpose is to be used as a primary key. A surrogate key would be an added field, such as a sequence of numbers called carID, which is not derived from the record data.

Find out the structure of the records that your bank uses for your bank-account data. One of the fields will be a surrogate key. Find out which field is the surrogate field and why it avoids problems that could arise if your name was used as the primary key.

DESIGN 2

ONE-TO-MANY RELATIONSHIP

The Dwarf entity and the other two entities named Product and Order illustrate one-to-many relationships between entities.

The Seven Dwarfs order items such as pickaxes and hats, which are stored in the Product entity. Each product has a primary key named "productID" and other details about the product.

Each order has a primary key named "orderID" to uniquely identify the order, and an attribute to store the date of the order. The "dwarfID" and "productID" attributes are used to link the Order entity to the Dwarf and Product entities respectively by placing their primary key in the Orders entity.

These key fields are called foreign keys in the Order entity, since they have travelled abroad to another table. The Dwarf entity and the Product entity are both linked to the Order entity in a one-to-many relationship.

The term "one-to-many" refers to the fact that one occurrence in the Dwarf entity can have many occurrences in the Order entity. Also, one occurrence in the Product entity can have many occurrences in the Order entity. The entity-relationship diagram below illustrates the relationships between the tables.

DON'T FORGET

There are three types of relationships between tables in a relational database which you will cover in your practical work in this course. These are one-to-one, one-to-many and many-to-many.

Entity: Course
courseID
description
fee
duration
college

MANY-TO-MANY RELATIONSHIP

A many-to-many relationship is a common relationship between two entities in a relational database. The example given below clarifies this type of relationship and the need for an extra entity that is placed between the two entities that are connected by the many-to-many relationship.

The Dwarf entity and another entity named Course illustrate a many-to-many relationship between entities. The dwarfs go on training courses for diamond-cutting, pickaxe skills, mine-tunnelling and so on, which are stored in rows of the Course entity shown here.

The Dwarf entity and the Course entity are linked in a many-to-many relationship. This is a many-to-many relationship because one occurrence in the Dwarf entity can have many occurrences in the Course entity. Also, one occurrence in the Course entity can have many occurrences in the Dwarf entity. In other words, a dwarf can do more than one course, and a course can be taken by more than one dwarf.

Many-to-many relationships are replaced with two one-to-many relationships by placing an extra entity between the two entities. In this case, the Signup entity is placed between the Dwarf and Course entities, and the dwarfID and courseID attributes are foreign keys which link the entities.

Entity: Dwarf	Entity: Signup	Entity: Course
dwarfID	signupID	courseID
dwarfname	dwarfID*	description
age	courseID*	fee
street	paid	duration
town		college
postcode		
married		

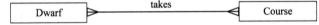

Other examples of two entities that are related in a many-to-many relationship could be an entity of athletes and an entity of events in a sports event, or an entity of students and an entity of classes in a school.

ENTITY-RELATIONSHIP DIAGRAM WITH ATTRIBUTES

Shown below is an entity-relationship diagram for the Dwarf, Product and Order entities.

The diagram shows the cardinality of the relationship and the attributes of each entity.

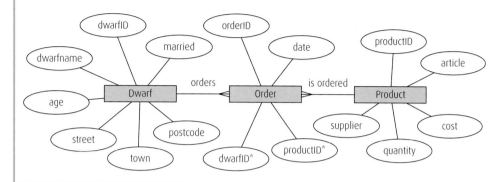

DON'T FORGET

A compound key is a type of primary key which uses a combination of two or more attributes to identify one, and only one, entity occurrence. In this example, the two foreign keys dwarfID and courseID in the Signup entity are used as a compound key. Neither of these foreign fields is unique in the occurrences in the Signup entity, but the combination of the two attributes is unique.

ENTITY-OCCURRENCE DIAGRAM

One way of identifying the relationships between entities is called an entity-occurrence diagram. This illustrates specific relationships between entities by giving instances of actual occurrences.

The following table indicates which dwarfs have signed up for which courses, and which courses have been signed up for by which dwarfs.

The entity-occurrence diagram below illustrates the occurrence in the table.

Dwarf	Course
D001	C02
D002	C01
D002	C07
D004	C01
D004	C03
D004	C05
D005	C03
D006	C02
D006	C07
D007	C04

Dwarf   **Course**

D001 ●	● C01
D002 ●	● C02
D003 ●	● C03
D004 ●	● C04
D005 ●	● C05
D006 ●	● C06
D007 ●	● C07

The lines between the entities show how the instances of each entity are linked.

The entity-occurrence diagram shows that one course can be taken by many dwarfs and that one dwarf can take many courses. This means that a many-to-many relationship exists between the Dwarf and Course entities.

ONLINE

Learn more about entity-occurrence diagrams by watching the YouTube video at www.youtube.com/watch?v=coyHTpu5XeU

ONLINE

How well have you learned this topic? Take the Design 2 test at www.brightredbooks.net

THINGS TO DO AND THINK ABOUT

Different schools use different software to implement the database requirements of this course. Ask your teacher to demonstrate the features provided with a variety of database software to create tables, queries and reports.

DESIGN 3

DATA DICTIONARY

A data dictionary lists the entities in a database, the attribute names, attribute type (text, number, date, time, Boolean), attribute size, validation details (presence-check, restricted choice, field length, range-check) and an identification of primary and foreign keys.

Entity	Attribute Name	PK/FK	Data Type	Data Size	Unique	Required	Validation	Sample Data
Dwarf	dwarfID	PK	Text	4	Y	Y		D005
	dwarfname		Text	12	Y	Y		Dopey
	age		Number		N	Y	>=0 and <=600	427
	street		Text	20	N	Y		Elm Street
	town		Text	20	N	Y		Chicago
	postcode		Text	8	N	N		CA12 8NY
	married		Boolean		N	Y	Restricted choice	Yes or No
Course	courseID	PK	Text	3	Y	Y		C02
	description		Text	30	Y	Y		Pickaxe skills
	fee		Number		N	Y	>=80 and <=130	115
	duration		Number		N	Y	>=1 and <=5	3
	college		Text	20	N	Y		St Ann's
Signup	signuptID	PK	Text	4	Y	Y		S267
	dwarfID	FK	Text	4	N	Y	Lookup from Dwarf table	D002
	courseID	FK	Text	3	N	Y	Lookup from Course table	C05
	paid		Boolean		N	Y	Restricted choice	Yes or No

QUERY DESIGN

The design of a query should include:

- the field(s) or calculated values that are required
- the table(s) required used to provide the results
- the search criteria to be used
- any grouping that is required
- any field/fields that are used to sort the data and the type/types of sort required.

Dwarf	Grumpy	Dwarf ID	4
Age	501		

Course	Fee (£)
Diamond-cutting	160.00
Mine-tunnelling	170.00
Advanced pickaxe skills	135.00

The report below displays the Name and Age of the dwarf whose DwarfID = 4 and the Description and Fee (£) for each course for which the dwarf has signed up.

It is produced by creating a query which has criteria for selecting the data and the required fields from the Dwarfs and Courses tables and then creating a report based upon the query.

Field(s) and calculation(s)	Dwarf.dwarfname, Dwarf.dwarfID, Dwarf.age, Course.description, Course.fee
Table(s) and query	Dwarf, Course
Search criteria	Dwarf.dwarfID = 4
Grouping	
Sort order	

DATABASE EXPRESSIONS AND AGGREGATE FUNCTIONS

Expressions

Expressions can be added to queries which perform calculations involving fields and values to provide extra data items.

The fees in dollars can be created by entering the expression below into the query.

Fee($): [Course.Fee] * 1·35

In this example, the expression is using an exchange rate of £1 = $1·35.

Aggregate Functions

Aggregate functions are used to perform calculations involving multiple records.

A SUM aggregate function can be used to calculate the total cost of all the courses in the report by adding up the values in the Fee($) column. The following formula can be placed in a Textbox in the Footer section of a report.

= SUM([Course.Fee] * 1·35)

There are other aggregate functions which can be used to return MAX, MIN, AVG etc.

The report can be created to display the number of articles that have been sold by each of the product suppliers, using the Product table shown below.

Products table				
Product ID	Article	Price (£)	Quantity	Supplier
1	Small pickaxe	79·99	9	MiningLand
2	Medium pickaxe	134·99	217	MiningLand
3	Large pickaxe	199·00	5	MiningLand
4	Soft hat (red)	24·99	80	The Headgear Company
5	Soft hat (blue)	24·99	80	The Headgear Company
6	Beard shampoo	2·95	56	Boots

The query shown below selects the Quantity and Supplier fields from the Product table, grouping them on the Supplier field and using a SUM aggregate function on the Quantity field to total the quantity of articles sold by each supplier.

The total quantities sold by each supplier are listed in increasing order.

Field(s) and calculation(s)	Supplier, SUM(Quantity)
Table(s) and query	Product
Search criteria	
Grouping	Supplier
Sort order	SUM(Quantity) ASC

A report based upon the query is then produced.

Supplier	SUM(Quantity)
Boots	56
The Headgear Company	160
MiningLand	231

THINGS TO DO AND THINK ABOUT

There is a specimen assignment task for this course which you can find at www.brightredbooks.net or download from the SQA website.

Study the requirements of the database part of this task. You will see that the database part of the coursework assignment asks you to identify the cardinality of the relationships between tables and to implement SQL code to perform a range of outputs using aggregate functions, sorting and wildcards.

ONLINE

You will probably need to use or create a data dictionary for the assignment part of the assessment for this course. Use this spread to familiarise yourself with this method of database design.

DON'T FORGET

ASC is used to sort a field in ascending order, and DESC is used to sort a field in descending order.

ONLINE TEST

Take the test on Design 3 at www.brightredbooks.net

SQL

INTRODUCTION

SQL stands for Structured Query Language (pronounced "sequel" or "S-Q-L").

The language is used to perform tasks such as updating data on a database, or retrieving data from a database. Standard SQL commands such as SELECT, INSERT, UPDATE or DELETE can be used to accomplish most tasks.

INSERT, DELETE, UPDATE, WHERE

The examples below use a table named "country" which has seven records.

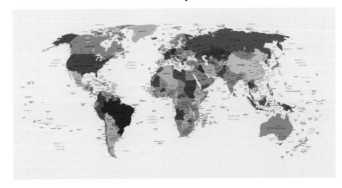

country				
country_id	name	continent	population	area_kmsq
1	Italy	Europe	64,762,320	301,308
2	Algeria	Africa	37,100,000	2,381,741
3	UK	Europe	58,667,840	242,900
4	Mexico	North America	107,027,504	1,958,201
5	Bhutan	Asia	38,394	749,090
6	France	Europe	51,495,667	551,500
7	Canada	North America	35,702,707	9,984,670

INSERT

The INSERT statement can be used to add records to a table.

In this example, a record for Denmark would be added to the country table.

INSERT INTO country (country_id, name, continent, population, area_kmsq)

VALUES (8, 'Denmark', 'Europe', 5634437, 43094);

UPDATE

The UPDATE statement can be used to change values in rows that already exist.

In this example, the population of France would be updated to a new value.

UPDATE country SET population = 54596008 WHERE country_id = 6;

DELETE

The DELETE statement can be used to remove rows from a table.

This example deletes the countries with a population of under 10 million from the Country table.

DELETE FROM country WHERE population < 10000000;

QUESTION 2

A data dictionary was created for the design of a college library's relational database. The data dictionary shown below lists the Author and Book entities and the details of their attributes.

State a suitable entry for each of the missing values A, B, C, D, E, F, G, H, I, J and K.

Entity name: Author

Attribute	Key	Type	Unique	Validation
authorID	PK	NUMBER	A	>=1 and <= 999
authorname		TEXT	B	C
sex		TEXT	N	Restricted choice (F, M)
email		TEXT	Y	Max length = 30

Entity name: Book

Attribute	Key	Type	Unique	Validation
bookID	PK	NUMBER	D	>=1 and <= 9,999
authorID*	E	NUMBER	F	G
title		TEXT	N	Max length = 40
hardback		BOOLEAN	N	H
genre		TEXT	I	Max length = 40
publisher		TEXT	N	J
publicationdate		DATE	N	K

QUESTION 3

When designing a relational database, it is essential to define the entities, their attributes and the cardinality between the entities making up the database.

(a) Explain the term "cardinality".

(b) Below is a brief description of seven different pairs of entities that are part of a relational database.

State whether each of the entities are related in a one-to-one, one-to-many or many-to-many relationship, and explain your answer.

A   Actors and films that they have appeared in

B   Headteachers and schools that they manage

C   Mothers and their children

D   Athletes and events in a sporting competition

E   Capital cities and countries in the world

(c) Direct many-to-many relationships between two entities cannot be implemented in a relational database.

Explain how a many-to-many relationship is resolved in a relational database.

(d) Entity-relationship diagrams and entity-occurrence diagrams are both used in the modelling of a relational database.

Describe the difference between an entity-relationship diagram and an entity-occurrence diagram.

DON'T FORGET

In the Computing Science Higher course, you can be asked to describe and illustrate a data dictionary with a minimum of three entities. The important thing is to be able to identify the entities' names, attribute names, primary and foreign keys, attribute types (text, number, date, time, Boolean), attribute size and validation (presence-check, restricted choice, field length, range).

DON'T FORGET

It is a common mistake for candidates to use commercial terms in their exam answers. Don't use the names of actual software items such as Microsoft Access, iTunes, Google etc. in the exam. Make sure that you use general terms such as database, entity, attribute, query, search engine etc.

 THINGS TO DO AND THINK ABOUT

Don't start your answer to a question by just repeating the question. This is not providing any of your own understanding of the question, and you are just wasting time, which is a scarce resource in an exam.

REVISION QUESTIONS 2

QUESTION 1

A bird-life club keeps a database which stores information on common British birds.

The bird-life club is interested in monitoring the populations of the birds in order to watch out for birds whose population is decreasing and threatened with extinction. The population has three possible values depending upon whether it is increasing, decreasing or stable. A table from the database is shown below.

birds			
bird_id	name	clutch_size	population
1	Robin	5	increasing
2	Wood pigeon	2	decreasing
3	Chaffinch	4	increasing
4	Blackbird	6	stable
5	Sparrow	4	increasing
6	Crow	4	decreasing
7	Magpie	6	stable
8	Goldfinch	4	stable
9	Blue tit	5	increasing
10	Wren	7	increasing
11	Swan	5	stable
12	Thrush	3	decreasing

(a) Explain the result of each of the following sections of SQL code.

   (i) UPDATE birds SET population = 'stable' WHERE bird_id = 2;

   (ii) INSERT INTO birds (bird_id, name, clutch_size, population)
        VALUES (13, 'Eagle', 2, 'stable');

   (iii) DELETE FROM birds WHERE clutch_size >= 6;

(b) Draw the results table for each of the following SQL statements.

   (i) SELECT name, clutch_size
       FROM birds
       WHERE clutch_size = 5 OR clutch_size= 6
       ORDER BY clutch_size DESC;

   (ii) SELECT name, clutch_size, population
        FROM birds
        WHERE name LIKE '%h';

QUESTION 2

(a) The SQL language uses two wildcard symbols, "%" and "_".

   (i) What is the purpose of a wildcard when used in SQL statements?

   (ii) Explain the difference between the "%" and the "_" symbols used in wildcards.

(b) A database named "countries" has a table with a field named "country_name".
    Describe the output of each of the following SQL queries.

   (i) SELECT country_name
       FROM countries
       WHERE country_name LIKE '%ya';

contd

(ii) SELECT country_name
FROM countries
WHERE country_name LIKE '_g%';

(c) The columns that are displayed when the queries are executed are not easy to make sense of. The "AS" keyword is used to make the columns more readable.

Explain the function of the "AS" keywords in the SQL statement shown below.

SELECT pet_id AS Pet, pet_species AS Species

QUESTION 3

This table contains 13 records on the percentage exam marks of a class of students in Maths, English and Art.

(a) (i) Explain the function of an SQL aggregate function.

(ii) Name two examples of aggregate functions.

(b) Copy and complete the tables shown below to show the result of these SQL queries.

(i) SELECT MIN(english)
FROM students

(ii) SELECT sex, MAX(art)
FROM students
GROUP BY sex

(iii) SELECT sex, COUNT(name)
FROM students
GROUP BY sex
ORDER BY COUNT(name) ASC;

(iv) SELECT sex, AVG(maths)
FROM students
GROUP BY sex
ORDER BY AVG(maths) DESC;

students					
student_id	name	sex	maths	english	art
1	Sam Higgins	M	63	68	53
2	Jack Beattie	M	76	64	90
3	Sally Watson	F	91	73	81
4	Phyllis Partridge	F	29	53	72
5	Andrew Green	M	71	76	65
6	Gwen Kirkwood	F	62	68	76
7	Mark O'Neil	M	57	43	39
8	Patricia Cairns	F	73	83	87
9	Sophie Rowand	F	88	75	60
10	Martin Porter	M	63	47	67
11	David Leith	M	59	56	57
12	Aaron Hawkins	M	73	71	81
13	Stephanie Banks	F	65	65	68

MIN(english)

sex	MAX(art)

sex	COUNT(name)

sex	AVG(maths)

THINGS TO DO AND THINK ABOUT

Create the database tables used in question 1 and question 3 in this spread.

It will take time to create and populate the bird and student tables before you can create and run the SQL queries. Work with a partner to share the load and to help each other with any problems that may arise.

Then answer the questions as practical tasks by entering the SQL code in the questions. Remember that once you run a query it will change the data in the database tables, so keep a copy of the original tables so that you can run each SQL query on the original data.

WEB DESIGN AND DEVELOPMENT

ANALYSIS AND DESIGN

ANALYSIS

Before a website is designed and developed, it is important to identify the skills and requirements of the end users of the website and also the functional requirements that the website is required to perform.

End-User Requirements

End users will vary in their age and IT skill levels. A website that is to be used by elderly people will require a different user interface from an interface that is designed for young people. A children's website would use a small amount of simple text, be colourful and use a lot of images and videos. In general, an adult's website would use more text and be more content-based, rather than be colourful for appeal to children.

Functional Requirements

The functional requirements of a website define the functions that the website is required to perform.

For example, the website may be required to create accounts, display images of products for sale, provide external hyperlinks to other websites and so on.

DESIGN

A simple website with a small number of pages can easily be created and maintained by one person. However, in a complex website containing hundreds or even thousands of pages in many sections and subsections, it must be carefully planned. Such websites are created by teams of web developers, and design is essential for consistency and communication between the developers.

Multi-Level Website

The structure of a website must be designed as well as the page content to ensure that users can easily find a particular page among what could be thousands of individual pages.

A simple website with a small number of pages can be navigated at one level by providing links from the home page to each of the other pages and back to the home page. However, in a more complex website with a large number of web pages, multi-level navigation is needed in which the user navigates through a hierarchy of sections and subsections.

DON'T FORGET

In this course, it is stated in the course specification that you may be required to describe a multi-level website with a home page and two additional levels, with no more than four pages per level.

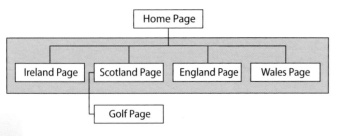

The structure of the navigation must be planned at the design stage to systematically group web pages and make the navigation through the hierarchical levels quick and usable for the end user.

There are lots of design notations used to demonstrate the navigational structure. The SQA will always use a shaded background to show the pages that are part of the horizontal navigational bar, which is at the top of each page in the site. The home page will be included in the navigational bar. The horizontal lines show the multi-links that link the web pages together. The vertical lines show the links that only go in one direction from top to bottom.

This diagram shows the navigational structure of a UK website, with horizontal navigation between the different countries, and vertical navigation that goes in one direction from the Scotland Page to the Golf Page.

WIREFRAME

A wireframe is used early in the development of software to provide a skeletal outline of the components of a program interface before detailing the specifics.

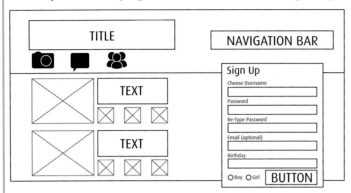

The design of a website interface will contain a wireframe for each of the pages in the website.

Using a wireframe to design the website interface improves the clarity and consistency of the interface across the different pages.

A wireframe should indicate the intended layout of the page and show the horizontal and vertical position of:

- navigational bars

- all text elements on the page

- any media elements (images, audio clips and video clips)

- elements that allow the user to interact with the page

- any form inputs.

This example shows a wireframe which indicates where images, text, navigation controls and command buttons are positioned. The details of the content of these elements of the program interface are not specified at this stage.

Media			
Text	TXT	RTF	DOC
Graphics	GIF	JPEG	PNG
Video	MP4	AVI	MOV
Sound	MP3	WAV	FLAC

Wire-framing should indicate the file formats of any media used in the web page (text, graphics, video and audio).

 **THINGS TO DO AND THINK ABOUT**

Visit the Football section of the BBC website, and consider how the designers of this website have provided internal navigation through this site from the Home page to the Football pages.

Ask yourself the following questions.

How easy is it to go from the Home page to the section on Football within the Sports section?

Are there image links as well as text hyperlinks to the section on Football?

Is there a search box that could be used to go straight to the Football section?

Try to draw a diagram to represent the navigational structure from the Home page to the Football section using the design notation described in this spread. Use shading to indicate the horizontal navigation bar, and use horizontal and vertical lines where appropriate.

 **DON'T FORGET**

The National 5 course covered some commonly used standard file formats for video files. You should at least know the ones that are listed in the table given here. Look over the National 5 book if you need to refresh your knowledge of these file formats and the types of compression that they use.

 ONLINE

Visit https://wireframe.cc, which is a website that allows you to create wireframe designs of your web pages.

 ONLINE TEST

Take the test on Analysis and Design at www.brightredbooks.net

IMPLEMENTATION (CSS) 1

INLINE, INTERNAL AND EXTERNAL CSS

CSS uses style sheets to define the formatting of elements of a web page by specifying colour, font, text alignment, size, borders, table sizes and so on.

It makes it easier to have consistent formatting in the pages of a website, since a style sheet has to be created only once and then used by any page that references the CSS file.

Inline CSS

An inline style sheet is used to apply a style to a single occurrence of an element. Inline style sheets are declared within individual tags and affect only those tags. Inline style sheets are declared with the style attribute.

Example:

```
<p style="color:blue; text-align:center;">This text is blue and centred.</p>
```
This example uses the style sheet commands "color" and "text-align" to denote that the text in a paragraph will be blue and centred. Output:

This text is blue and centred.

Internal CSS

An internal style sheet is embedded within the HTML code of each web page. A website with a large number of pages would require internal style sheets to be placed on every page where they are used.

It is defined using the <style> and </style> tags and is placed in the <head> section. The <style> tag specifies the content type of a style sheet with its type attribute, which should be set to "text/css".

```
<style type="text/css">

    CSS style rules go here

</style>
```

Example:

```
<html>
    <head>
        <style>
            h1
            {
            font-family:Times New Roman;
            color: purple;
            }
            p
            {
            font-family:Harrington;
            color: blue;
            font-size: 18px;
            }
        </style>
    </head>
    <body>
        <h1>This text uses Times New Roman font and is purple.</h1>
        <p>This text is in Harrington font, blue and 18 font size.</p>
    </body>
</html>
Output:
```
This text uses Times New Roman font and is purple.

This text is in Harrington font, blue and 18 font size.

DON'T FORGET

The format of CSS rules and the definitions for inline, internal and external CSS are commonly asked for in assessments. In the practical assignment for your coursework, you are allowed to use resources and do not need to know the format by heart, but you will need to learn the exact format of these CSS instructions for the exam.

DON'T FORGET

The term "cascading" is used to describe the fact that changes to a style sheet will cascade through to all of the web pages that are based on that style sheet.

contd

External CSS

An external style sheet is declared in a separate file with a ".css" extension.

Web pages can then link to the external file to use the CSS rules in the style sheet.

External style sheets are called using the <link> tag, which is placed in the <head> section.

The link to an external style sheet is described by three attributes:

- rel – An external style sheet has this attribute set to the value "stylesheet"
- type – An external style sheet on a web page has this attribute set to the value "text/css"
- href – States the name and location of the external style sheet to be used.

```
Style1.css

h2
{
font-family: Arial;
font-size: 16px;
font-weight: bold;
}
```

Example:

```
<html>
    <head>
        <link rel="stylesheet" type="text/css" href="Style1.css">
    </head>
    <body>
        <h2>This text is Arial font, 16-pixel font size and bold.</h2>
    </body>
</html>
```

Output:

This text is Arial font, 16-pixel font size and bold.

GROUPING AND DESCENDANT SELECTORS

Selectors can be used in CSS as separate elements, or can be grouped together with grouping selectors, or can inherit rules in descendant selectors.

Grouping Selectors

CSS allows properties and rules to be set for more than one selector at the same time. Each selector is separated by columns and then followed by the CSS rules.

The following example will apply the CSS rules for colour and text alignment to the h1, h2 and p selectors.

Example:

```
h1, h2, p {color: Maroon; text-align: center;}
```

Descendant Selectors

A descendant selector matches all of the elements that are descendants of an ancestor element.

The first selector represents the ancestor element, which is a structurally superior element followed by a space; and then the second selector represents the descendant element.

The following example will apply the CSS rules for font size, background colour and text alignment to the <p> selectors that are placed inside the <div> selector.

Example:

```
div p {font-size: 24px; background-color: yellow; text-align: center;}
```

THINGS TO DO AND THINK ABOUT

Try out the examples of inline, internal and external style sheets used in this spread by entering the code into a text editor such as Notepad or WordPad.

Once you have entered the code, edit the code to try out different formatting for font, colour, alignment and so on.

ONLINE

Visit www.inmotionhosting.com and use the search box to explore further the use of inline, internal and external CSS.

DON'T FORGET

Maintenance is easiest with external style sheets, since updating the external CSS will automatically apply to every web page that is linked to it.

ONLINE TEST

Take the test on Implementation (CSS) 1 at www.brightredbooks.net

IMPLEMENTATION (CSS) 2

APPEARANCE AND POSITIONING

The following CSS properties are used to control the appearance and positioning of HTML elements:

- margins, borders, padding
- sizes (height, width)
- display (block, inline, none)
- float (left, right)
- clear (both)

Margins, Borders and Padding

HTML elements can be considered as boxes when describing their design and layout.

The CSS box model consists of margins, borders, padding and the actual content itself.

Margin
The margin is a white space area around the outside of an element. The margin property is used to create a gap between the element and other adjacent elements.

Border
The border property is used to create a boundary that goes around the padding and content. The thickness of the border is usually specified in pixels.

Padding
The padding is a white-space area inside the edge of the element. The padding property is used to push content in from the edge of the element.

Content
The content property of the box is where content such as images and text appears.

Example:
The following example defines CSS margin, border and padding rules for a div element.
```
div {margin: 20px; border: 15px; padding: 20px;}
```

Sizes (Height, Width)

The height and width properties are used to define the size of an element. This can be applied to the body element to set a fixed width for all pages in a website.

Example:
The following CSS rule can be used to set the width of each web page to 800px.
```
body{width: 900px;}
```

It is common to set the height of the header, nav and footer elements to a fixed size, which improves the consistency of the pages in the website.

Example:
The following CSS rules can be used to set the height of the header, nav and footer elements.
```
header {height: 100px;} footer {height: 80px;} nav {height: 400px;}
```

Display (Block, Inline, None)

Most HTML elements have a default display value of block, inline or none, which specifies how an element is to be displayed.

- display: block; an element takes up the entire width of its container
- display: inline; an element takes up only as much room as it requires
- display: none; the element is not visible, and the space that would have been taken collapses.

contd

Float (Left, Right) and Clear (both)

The float property is used for the positioning of elements on web pages. For example, an image can be positioned to float to the right of a text element so that the text wraps around the left side of the image. Left makes the element float to the left of its container; right makes the element float to the right of its container.

Example 1:

The CSS rules for the img element will float the cat image to the left of the p element text.
```
img {
        width: 880px;
        height: 570px;
        margin-right: 20px;
        float: left;
}
```
This image has its float property set to left, which makes the image float to the left of the web page and the text in the paragraph wraps around the right side of the image.

Example 2:

The CSS rules for the img element will float the cat image to the right of the p element text.
```
img {
        width: 880px;
        height: 570px;
        margin-right: 20px;
        float: right;
}
```

This image has its float property set to right, which makes the image float to the right of the web page and the text in the paragraph wraps around the left side of the image.

Clear (both)

The clear property is used to clear the effect of floating elements on subsequent elements.

Example:

The following CSS rule is used to ensure that the <nav> and <main> elements start a new line and remain unaffected by any float properties applied elsewhere in the page.
```
nav, main {display: block; clear: both;}
```

ONLINE

Visit w3schools.com and research the display and float properties further. Investigate more properties that are used in the appearance and positioning of web pages.

HORIZONTAL NAVIGATION BARS

The <nav> element can be used to act as a container for an unordered list of hyperlinks which are displayed as bullet points.

```
<nav>
<ul>
    <li><a href="home.html">Home</a></li>
    <li><a href="tennis.html">Tennis</a></li>
    <li><a href="golf.html">Golf</a></li>
    <li><a href="athletics.html">Athletics</a></li>
</ul>
</nav>
```

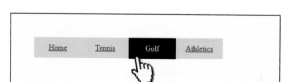

To format the list into a horizontal navigation bar requires CSS rules.

```
nav ul {list-style-type: none;}
```
```
nav ul li {float: left; width: 100px; text-align: center;}
```
```
nav ul li a {display: block; padding: 12px; background-color: lightblue;}
```
```
nav ul li a:hover {background-color: #000; color: White;}
```

ONLINE TEST

Take the test on Implementation (CSS) 2 at www.brightredbooks.net

 THINGS TO DO AND THINK ABOUT

Create a simple website with a header, nav, main and footer section. Try out the appearance and positioning of CSS properties described in this spread. Edit the CSS code, and see how it affects the appearance of the website.

IMPLEMENTATION (HTML) 1

HTML STRUCTURAL ELEMENTS

Most websites have an overall structure to the HTML content, with distinct sections within the page. A typical page follows the basic structure shown here.

Header
The header element contains the top-level heading of the page, with items such as a title, company logo, etc.

Navigation
The navigation element is often placed under the header element and contains the navigation bar and links.

Main
The main element holds the main content of the web page and may be further divided into subsections using the <section> or <div> tags.

Section
The section element is used to create sections within the document. Typically, this will be used to divide the main element into subsections.

Footer
The footer element goes across the bottom of the site and contains secondary information such as copyright information, contact details and legal agreements.

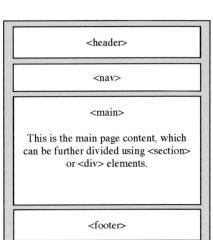

DON'T FORGET

The header, nav, main, section, div and footer elements are used to create a web page with a structure that has distinct sections.

DON'T FORGET

The content of a <main> element should be unique to a web page. Content that is repeated across several web pages, such as navigation bars, copyright information, site logos etc., should not be included in the <main> element.

HTML CODE

The web page shown below demonstrates a typical use of HTML structural elements in the page layout of a web page.

```
<html>

<head>
        <title>Favourite Apples</title>
        <style>
            .mystyle {border: 1px solid black; background-color: lightblue;}
            .mysection {border: 1px solid blue; background-color: aliceblue;}
        </style>
</head>

<body>
        <header class="mystyle">
        <h1 align="center">*****
        <image width="400" height="140" src="MyImage.gif">******</h1>
        <h1 align="center">How do you like them apples?</h1>
        </header>

        <nav class="mystyle">
            <ul>
            <li><a href="home.html">Home</a></li>
            <li><a href="reddelicious.html">Red Delicious</a></li>
            <li><a href="grannysmith.html">Granny Smith</a></li>
            <li><a href="braeburn.html">Braeburn</a></li>
            </ul>
        </nav>
```

contd

```
        <main class="mystyle">
        <h1>The three apples described below are
commonly found in supermarkets.</h1>

        <section class="mysection">
        <h2>Red Delicious</h2>
        <p>These bright red apples are sweet and usually
quite large.
        <image width="50" height="50" src="Red
Delicious.gif"></p>
        </section>

        <section class="mysection">
        <h2>Granny Smith</h2>
        <p>These juicy, green apples make a great filling
for apple pies.
        <image width="50" height="50"
src="Granny Smith.gif"></p>
        </section>

        <section class="mysection">
        <h2>Braeburn</h2>
        <p>These firm, red/orange apples are cool and refreshing.
        <image width="50" height="50" src="Braeburn.gif"></p>
        </section>
        <h1>Try these apples sometime. You won't regret it!</h1>
        </main>

        <footer class="mystyle">
                <p>Contact:
                <a href="mailto:rottencore@hotmail.com">rottencore@hotmail.com</a>.</p>
                <p>Telephone: 07756 007007
        </footer>
</body>

</html>
```

The page preview on the right shows:

How do you like them apples?

- Home
- Red Delicious
- Granny Smith
- Braeburn

The three apples described below are commonly found in supermarkets.

Red Delicious

These bright red apples are sweet and usually quite large.

Granny Smith

These juicy, green apples make a great filling for apple pies.

Braeburn

These firm, red orange apples are cool and refreshing.

Try these apples sometime. You won't regret it!

Contact rottencore@hotmail.com
Telephone: 07756 007007

Structure labels (right margin): `<header>`, `</header>`, `<nav>`, `</nav>`, `<main>`, `<section>`, `</section>`, `<section>`, `</section>`, `<section>`, `</section>`, `</main>`, `<footer>`, `</footer>`

ID Attribute

The structural elements in a web page, such as header and main, can be given an ID attribute to format a specific structural element of a page with CSS rules or to manipulate the element with JavaScript.

Example:

A JavaScript function then uses this ID to change the text of the h1 element to "Welcome to our website!" when the button is clicked.

```
<html>
<body>

<h1 id="myWelcome">WELCOME</h1>
<button onclick="myFunction()">Click me</button>

<script>
function myFunction () {
document.getElementById("myWelcome").innerHTML = "Welcome to our website!";
}
</script>

</body>
</html>
```

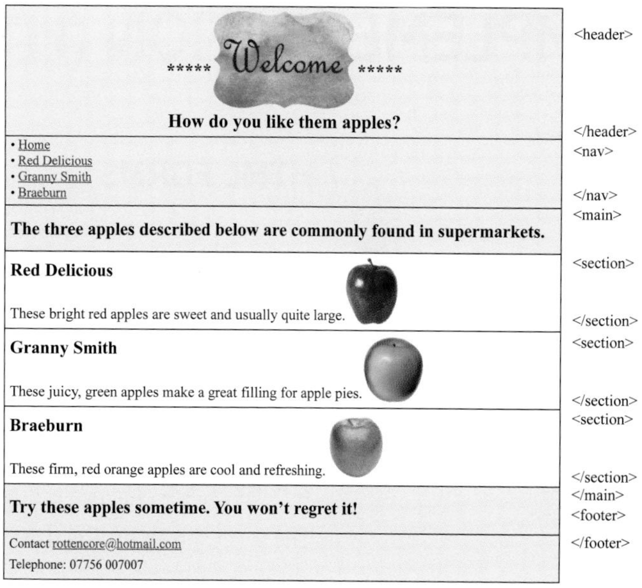

DON'T FORGET

HTML is not a static language but continues to develop through progressive versions. HTML 5 introduced the header, nav, main, section and footer elements to define different areas of a web page.

ONLINE

Visit the website https://www.w3schools.com/html/html5_new_elements.asp to explore further the page-layout tags described in this spread.

ONLINE TEST

Take the test on Implementation (HTML) 1 at www.brightredbooks.net

 THINGS TO DO AND THINK ABOUT

Enter the code for the "Favourite Apples" web page into a text editor such as Notepad or WordPad to practise the header, nav, main, section and footer structural elements.

IMPLEMENTATION (HTML) 2

HTML FORMS

Many websites have forms that allow users to enter and submit data. For example, a form may be used to collect a user's personal data to register an account or to enter data to search for a company's products.

An HTML <form> element is used to define a form, which enters input from the user.

The input elements are placed between the opening form tag and the closing form tag.

EXAMPLE

The form shown here is used by users of an ice-cream website to place online orders.

Ice Cream Orders

Customer name:

Address:

Telephone:

Number of cartons:

Choose your carton size: ○ Small ○ Medium ○ Large

Select flavour: Strawberry Mix ▾

Enter any extras here.

Send

The HTML code for the form is shown below.

```
<form>
Customer name:<br>
<input type="text" name="customername" size="25" maxlength="25" required><br>
Address:<br>
<input type="text" name="address" size="30" maxlength="30" required><br>
Telephone:<br>
<input type="text" name="telephone" size="15" maxlength="11" required><br>
<br><br>

Number of cartons:
<input type="number" name="cartons" min="6" max="24" required>
<br><br>

Choose your carton size:
<input type="radio" name="size" value="Small"> Small
<input type="radio" name="size" value="Medium"> Medium
<input type="radio" name="size" value="Large"> Large
<br><br>

Select flavour:
<select name="flavour">
<option value="Strawberry Mix">Strawberry Mix</option>
```

contd

```
<option value="Vanilla Pie">Vanilla Pie</option>
<option value="Crushed Meringue">Crushed Meringue</option>
</select>
<br><br>

<textarea name="extras" rows="3" cols="55">Enter any extras here.</textarea>
<br><br>

<input type="submit" onclick="alert('Form Entered')" value="Send">
</form>
```

Each of the six types of input elements used in the form is described below.

input type="text"

The customer name, address and telephone are each entered with a "text" input type.

The "type" attribute identifies the input element as a text.
The "name" attribute is used to identify the data when processed on a server by a server-side script. (The processing of the data by a server-side script is beyond the requirements of this course.)
The "size" attribute specifies the width of the text box when displayed in a browser.
The "maxlength" attribute sets a length-check to limit the number of characters that are entered.
The "required" attribute checks that the data is present.

input type="number"

The number of cartons is entered with a "number" input type.

The "type" attribute identifies the input element as a number.
The "name" attribute is used to identify the data when processed on a server by a server-side script.
The "min" and "max" attributes set a range-check by specifying the smallest and largest number that can be entered.
The "required" attribute performs a presence-check on the input.

input type="radio"

The choice of small, medium or large cartons is entered with a "radio" input type.

The "type" attribute identifies the input element as a radio button. The "name" attribute is used to identify the data when processed on a server by a server side script. The "value" attribute is used to give the element a value when the page loads.

select

The choice of flavour is selected from a list of input choices in a drop-down list. The items in the list are placed in option tags.

input type="textarea"

The customer can enter extended text for any required extras in a "textarea" input type. The "rows" and "columns" attributes are used to specify the width and height of the textarea element. Length- and presence-checks can be set in the same way as a text input type.

input type="submit"

The customer submits the form data to be processed by clicking on a submit button.

 THINGS TO DO AND THINK ABOUT

HTML forms have several elements for entering text, which include "text" and "textarea".

Investigate the "password" input type and find out how it differs from the "text" input type.

 **DON'T FORGET**

The **text** input type is used to enter one line of text, whereas the **textarea** input type is used to enter one or more lines of text. Both of these ways of entering text can have a length- and presence-check applied.

 ONLINE

Visit w3schools.com and research further the HTML form elements described in this spread. Investigate other attributes used by HTML form elements in addition to the ones required for this course.

 ONLINE TEST

Take the test on Implementation (HTML) 2 at www.brightredbooks.net

IMPLEMENTATION (JAVASCRIPT)

JAVASCRIPT MOUSE EVENTS

Scripts can contain instructions to be executed in response to certain mouse actions such as clicking a command button, moving the mouse pointer over or away from an image, or selecting an item from a drop-down list.

JavaScript uses the onmouseover, onmouseout and onclick events to make web content interactive. These events are implemented by placing the mouse event inside the HTML element according to the syntax shown below:

<img onmouseover=" ">

The action to be executed when the event occurs is placed inside the inverted commas.

Example 1
The following example uses the onmouseover and onmouseout mouse events to change the colour of an h1 heading. The colour of the h1 heading changes to red when the mouse pointer moves over it and changes to blue when the mouse moves away.

```
<html>
<head>
 <title>Rainbow City</title>
</head>

<body>
        <h1 onmouseover="style.color='red'" onmouseout="style.color='blue'">Change my colour</h1>
</body>
</html>
```

Example 2
The following example uses the onmouseover and onmouseout mouse events to change the image that is displayed when the mouse pointer moves over or away from an image element.

Each function is passed the img element as a parameter using "this".

The first function changes the src for the image to a sad image, and the second function changes the src for the image to a happy image.

Hello, here is a happy picture.

Move the mouse over the image and then away.

Hello, here is a happy picture.

Move the mouse over the image and then away.

contd

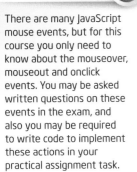

DON'T FORGET

There are many JavaScript mouse events, but for this course you only need to know about the mouseover, mouseout and onclick events. You may be asked written questions on these events in the exam, and also you may be required to write code to implement these actions in your practical assignment task.

DON'T FORGET

YouTube is a good place to look for further examples of JavaScript tutorials on mouseover, mouseout and onclick events – but remember that JavaScript is a very large and complex language, so restrict yourself to the events required for this course.

```
<html>
<head>
    <title>Mood Swings</title>
</head>
<body>
    <h1>Hello, here is a happy picture.</h1>
    <img onmouseover="sad(this)" onmouseout="happy(this)"
src="HappyPic.bmp">
    <p>Move the mouse over the image and then away.</p>

    <script>
        function sad(x) {
        x.src = "SadPic.bmp";
        }
        function happy(x) {
        x.src = "HappyPic.bmp";
        }
    </script>
</body>
</html>
```

Example 3
The following example uses the onclick mouse event to make the text in a p element visible when an image is clicked.

When the web page is initially loaded, a paragraph element is hidden by applying a CSS class that uses the rule display "none;" which makes the p element invisible.

The image element uses an onclick event that uses the ID of a paragraph element to execute the action "display='block'". This action makes the p element visible on the page.

```
<html>
<head>
    <title>Jokes World</title>
    <style>
        .hidden{display: none;}
    </style>
</head>

<body style="background-color:lightblue; font-size:24px;">
    <p>Why did a night club on Mars close down?</p>
    <img class="show" src="Punchline.bmp"
    onClick="document.getElementById('show').style.display='block'">
    <p id="show" class="hidden">Nobody came because there was no atmosphere!</p>
</body>
</html>
```

The web page when it loads is shown to the right.

After "Punchline" has been clicked, the text in the second paragraph is made visible.

THINGS TO DO AND THINK ABOUT
Try out the three examples of JavaScript used in this spread by entering the code into a text editor such as Notepad or WordPad.

ONLINE TEST

Take the test on Implementation (JavaScript) at www.brightredbooks.net

TESTING AND EVALUATION

TESTING

The purpose of testing website is to identify and rectify errors.

Testing should not be random but should be organised according to a test plan that uses appropriate criteria for the solution to be tested against. The test results should be documented with hard copy or electronic evidence.

Website testing will include:

- checking that the user interface and usability are suitable for the target users
- checking that input validation works correctly
- checking that all levels of navigation work
- checking that all internal and external hyperlinks work
- checking that text, graphics and videos display properly and that sound files work properly
- checking that the website is compatible with the device type and browser
- checking that scripts work correctly.

DON'T FORGET

For the coursework assignment, you may well be asked to test a website that you have created. Make sure that you have evidence of test results with screen shots and any other required documentation.

USABILITY TESTING

Usability testing measures the capacity of target users of a website to meet its intended purpose. Users can be asked to perform given tasks under controlled conditions to determine how quickly and error-free they can perform the tasks.

For example, users can be asked to navigate around certain pages of a website and enter some specified data. The number of clicks, time taken and number of errors can be recorded. Users can also be given post-test questionnaires to provide their feedback on the usability of the software.

The testers may be given:

- a persona — the tester takes on the role of a user of a certain age or experience
- test cases — the tester is given a set of actions to carry out a particular feature or function of the website
- scenarios — the tester is asked to use the website to perform a task such as registering an account or booking a ticket.

COMPATIBILITY TESTING

Websites undergo compatibility testing to ensure that they work properly in their intended environment. This type of testing is carried out to determine how well a website performs in a particular environment that includes the type of devices it is to be run on, the operating system and the web browser.

Device Type

The devices that are to display the website will have a specification that includes processor, RAM and storage capacity. It is important to do test runs in order to make sure that the hardware is sufficient to run the software efficiently and without crashing.

contd

Tablet, smartphone and desktop computers have very different specifications and sizes of screen from each other, and it is important to test that the website works correctly on the devices on which it will be used. For example, a website with a large amount of text that is appropriate to be displayed on a desktop computer might not be suitable for the small screen of a smartphone. Navigation is very important, and it must be considered whether the type of navigation is suitable for the device type, since using a keyboard and mouse to navigate is very different compared to using a touchscreen.

Browser

One issue for a website is to test it in as many browsers as possible. Each browser interprets the coding for a website in a slightly different manner, which means that the website can appear different when displayed in different browsers.

The appearance and functionality of the website should be viewed on multiple browsers to make sure that all of the features and functions behave as they are supposed to.

ONLINE

Learn more about website usability by watching the YouTube video at www.youtube.com/watch?v=0SyRjjAGpvg&t=119sx

EVALUATION

When the website development from analysis through to testing is completed, it is important to evaluate it in terms of whether or not the original requirements have been met. Very often, the client is not happy with the final product, and so this stage is important to rectify as many weaknesses as possible in the software before it is delivered in its final form.

Fitness for Purpose

A website is fit for purpose if it solves the problem that it is supposed to solve by meeting the functional requirements.

Test results for input validation, navigation links and media displays should be used to evaluate how good the website is at meeting the end-user requirements.

Usability

Even if the website is fit for purpose in terms of the functions that it performs, it might still be poor in terms of usability for the end users.

Usability test results recording the time taken to complete tasks and the error rate should be employed to evaluate the usability of the website solution.

 ## THINGS TO DO AND THINK ABOUT

Ask other members of your class to test the functionality and usability of a website that you have created. You may find that the software is not as usable as you had thought! It may not be as obvious to other people how to use the software as it is to you, since you were the one who created the website.

Make up a questionnaire with questions such as "Was it easy to navigate around the website?", "Was the interface consistent and clear?", "Was it possible to enter invalid data?" and so on.

 ONLINE TEST

Take the test on Testing and Evaluation at www.brightredbooks.net

REVISION QUESTIONS 1

QUESTION 1

A primary school requires a website to teach simple arithmetic to their youngest classes.

A website-development company has arranged a meeting at the school with the teachers to perform an analysis of the school's requirements.

(a) Suggest how the visual layout and readability of the user-interface design should be considered to take into account the end-user requirements.

(b) After the meeting, the development company creates a wireframe design of the website screens, which is then shown to the teachers in the school.

What are the advantages of creating the wireframe designs?

(c) The final website contains 16 web pages.

The website structure is multi-level, with a home page and two additional levels.

(i) Why might this website structure be unsuitable for the target users?

(ii) Suggest a more suitable structure for the website that takes account of the intended end users.

(d) The school uses the Google Chrome browser, since it finds that this is easier than other browsers for young children to use.

When the developers are testing the website, they use a browser called Mozilla Firefox.

Explain why problems might be caused by testing the website using a different browser from the one used by the school.

(e) The completed website is tested by the teachers, who are delighted with the navigation and usability of the website.

Suggest why further testing should be carried out to evaluate whether the website solution is fit for purpose.

DON'T FORGET

Wireframes are used commonly in this course as the main method of designing the pages in a website. You can expect a wireframe to be used in the coursework assignment to illustrate the design of a web page/website that you have to implement, or you may be asked to create your own wireframe design based on the user and functional requirements.

QUESTION 2

A broadcasting company is developing a sports website which will provide live scores of worldwide sporting events.

(a) Describe how each of these elements of the website should be tested:

- navigation bars
- input into text boxes
- media.

(b) During the testing stage, the website was tested on a desktop computer. Explain why simply testing the website on one type of device is inadequate.

(c) The testers decided to use Google Chrome when testing the website. Explain why the browser used during the testing phase must be taken into consideration.

(d) Tests were made to check that all of the media elements in the website displayed/played correctly. Explain why the choice of file formats of the media (text, graphics, video and audio) is important when implementing the website.

QUESTION 3

An airline company has a website where users can book flights.

When booking flights, the customers must enter a departure airport, destination airport, departure date, return date, the number of passengers and the class (economy, business, first).

Part of the booking web page is shown below.

 **DON'T FORGET**

Testing a website is not just about testing the functions that the website carries out, such as links, input validation and whether media files display properly. Testing also includes assessing the usability of the website in terms of how quickly the users can perform tasks and reducing their error rate.

(a) (i) Explain the term "usability" when applied to the interface for a website.

(ii) When users enter a letter into the "Departure airport" field, the screen responds as shown below.

Comment on the usability of this aspect of the web page.

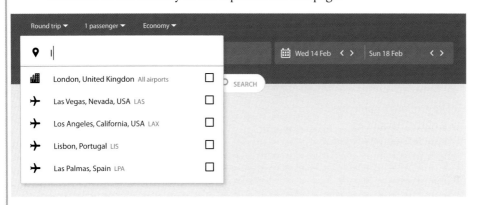

(b) The first version of the website required the users to type in the departure and return dates for a flight, which caused problems.

The improved web page shown above uses a date-picker to enter the departure and return dates.

Describe two ways in which a date-picker can improve the usability of the web page compared to typing the date.

(c) Part of the booking process requires the class of travel to be entered (economy, business, first).

Describe how the entering of the class could be achieved, and evaluate the usability of your solution.

(d) Recently, the airline company has had feedback from a number of users stating that they had difficulty in finding what they were looking for on the website.

They also felt that it was time-consuming and easy to make errors when entering data.

Describe how the airline company can test the usability of the website.

 THINGS TO DO AND THINK ABOUT

Remember that the SQA exam papers and practice papers made up by educational companies include a detailed marking scheme which provides model answers to the questions. You should take time to read the marking schemes thoroughly, since they are a good source of what is expected in a good answer.

REVISION QUESTIONS 2

QUESTION 1

Grouping and descendant selectors are used with CSS rules to improve the efficiency of Cascading Style Sheets code.

(a) Describe the terms "grouping selectors" and "descendant selectors".

(b) Apart from improving the efficiency of code, describe another advantage of using grouping and descendant selectors in CSS code.

QUESTION 2

A chess website is used to run online competitions between schools in the United Kingdom. Players can register online for the competitions using an HTML form.

The example below shows a student called Sally Higgens, who attends Arbroath Academy, entering her details.

(a) Complete the code below for the input elements used to enter the student's name by filling in missing parts A, B and C.

(The student's name has a length-check of 25 characters and a presence-check.)

```
<input type="___A___"
name="student" size="30"___
B___="25"___C___>
```

(b) Explain the difference between a "text" and a "textarea" input type.

Chess Registration Form

Student name:
`Sally Higgens`
School:
`Arbroath Academy`

Age: `15`

Standard: ○ Beginner ◉ Intermediate ○ Advanced

Select country: `England ▼`
England
Northern Island
Scotland
Wales

`Enter any add    ion here.`

`Submit`

(c) The online chess competitions are only for schools in the UK, and the players must enter their country as England, Northern Ireland, Scotland or Wales.

The code for the selection of the country is shown below. The code has three errors. Rewrite the code with the errors corrected.

```
Select country:
<select value="country">
<option value="England">England</option>
<option value="Northern Island">Northern Ireland</option>
<option valve="Scotland">Scotland</option>
<option value="Wales">Wales</option>
<select>
```

(d) The competition is open to students who are between 12 and 18 years old. Write the code for the input element for the age. (Your answer should validate that the age entered is in the range 12 to 18 and must be entered.)

(e) The chess players are asked to enter their standard: write the code to enter the student's standard from the choices given in the form (Beginner, Intermediate, Advanced).

(f) What happens when the student clicks on the "Submit" button?

QUESTION 3

A quiz website asks the user a question and then displays the solution when the user clicks on a solution image. The code for the web page is given below, with missing parts A, B and C.

```
<html>
<head>
      <title>Top Quiz</title>
      <style>
            .invisible{___A___}
      </style>
</head>
      <body style="background-color:lightred; font-size:36px;">
      <p>How many legs have 6 cows, 8 wasps and 3 spiders?</p>
      <img class="visible" src="Solution Image.bmp"
      onClick="document.getElementById('visible').style.display='block'">
      <p id="___B___" class="___C___">Ninety legs.</p>
</body>
</html>
```

Loaded web page:

Web page after the image is clicked:

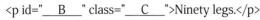

(a) Complete the code by entering the rule for the CSS class named ".invisible".

   .invisible{___A___}

(b) Complete the code for the second p element.

   <p id="___B___" class="___C___">Ninety legs.</p>

 ## THINGS TO DO AND THINK ABOUT

Practise your HTML form and JavaScript code by writing the code for the HTML form used in question 2 and the JavaScript code used in question 3 in this spread.

For the HTML form in question 2, write code to enter all the required data fields, and use appropriate validation checks for length, range and presence. Think about another suitable field that you could add to the form, and add code to implement it with suitable validation of the input data.

For the quiz website in question 3, make sure that the JavaScript works properly, and then edit the code to ask a different question and to give the appropriate solution.

COURSE ASSESSMENT

THE EXAM

INTRODUCTION

The course assessment consists of an exam paper and a practical assignment. The exam is allocated 110 marks out of a total of 160 for the course assessment.

Therefore, the exam makes up approximately 69% of the total marks for this course.

The exam covers the four mandatory areas, listed below.

The question is set and marked by the SQA and is sat in centres under the exam conditions specified by the SQA.

Course Assessment Structure
Component 1   Exam Paper: 110 marks
Component 2   Assignment: 50 marks
Total: 160 marks

THE EXAM

The time allocation for the exam is 2 hours 30 minutes.

The marks in the exam are distributed across all four areas of study in the percentages shown below:

- Software Design and Development   (approximately 40%)
- Computer Systems   (approximately 10%)
- Database Design and Development   (approximately 25%)
- Web Design and Development   (approximately 25%)

There are two sections in the question paper. You are required to answer all the questions in both sections.

Section 1   25 marks
This section has short-answer questions that test your knowledge and understanding of the topics listed in the syllabus across the four areas of the course.

Section 2   85 marks
This section has extended-response questions that test your ability to apply your knowledge and understanding in a challenging problem-solving context from across the four areas of the course.

Total: 110 marks

The exam has 110 marks to tackle in 2½ hours. Allowing 10 minutes for checking, you have an average of 1 minute to obtain each mark. Use this to pace yourself. You want to strike a balance between finishing the exam too quickly and running out of time halfway through the paper. Finishing the exam far too early usually means that you have not given fully explained and detailed answers. You should be finishing Section 1 in around 25 minutes. It is also a good idea to leave yourself a few minutes at the end of the exam to check over your answers.

A SPECIMEN PAPER IS AVAILABLE WHICH WILL GIVE YOU AN INDICATION OF THE LEVEL OF DIFFICULTY AND STYLE OF QUESTION THAT YOU CAN EXPECT IN THE ACTUAL EXAM.

Old exam papers from before 2018 are still a good source of revision for this course, since the majority of the content is still part of the new course.

Your teacher should be able to give you copies of these papers, or you can download them from the SQA website – but ask your teacher which questions are valid and which questions are not. It is good preparation to work through them, as they will give you a feel for the exam. It is also a good idea to look at the marking schemes, where you will find worked answers that will give you an indication of the content and the detail that are expected in your answers.

There are companies that create imitation exam papers in the same structure and style as the official SQA exams. These are a useful source of revision for your exam. Don't worry if a few of the questions are "over the top" in terms of level of difficulty or appear to be outside the course syllabus. This is simply because they are not official papers and have not been thoroughly checked in the same way as an SQA exam.

Ask your teacher where you can obtain imitation exam papers, or to clarify any points about which questions are valid.

You should see this book as an excellent way of consolidating the theory topics covered in class. If you thoroughly learn the content of this book, then you will have a strong foundation from which to tackle the exam. Remember that you can also use the online Bright Red Digital Zone for extra preparation. Your teacher is also a valuable resource for guidance and preparation and can be a source of extra questions and revision materials, or can at least provide information on where to find them for yourself.

DON'T FORGET

Curriculum for Excellence has been developed to create independent learners. Be prepared for an exam that tests your problem-solving abilities and not simply the ability to memorise and regurgitate facts.

ONLINE

The SQA exams start in April and continue through to the beginning of June. Months before the exams start, the exam timetable is published on the SQA website, where you can download your own personalised exam timetable.

THINGS TO DO AND THINK ABOUT

Each year, the SQA produces an examiner's report, which can be found on the SQA website. This report gives helpful comments on strong and weak areas of student performance and cut-off scores for each grade. This report can give you useful advice about the assessment process. It highlights common pitfalls in the coursework assignment as well as the exam, and gives advice on how to avoid areas where candidates tend to perform badly.

THE ASSIGNMENT

INTRODUCTION

The practical assignment is allocated 50 marks out of a total of 160 for the course assessment. Therefore, the practical coursework makes up 31% of the total marks for this course, and a good mark in this component can go a long way towards overall success.

Time

You are given an 8-hour time limit to complete the assignment.

The assignment covers three of the four areas of study:

- Software Design and Development
- Database Design and Development
- Web Design and Development.

The Computer Systems area of study is more concerned with theory than with practical work, and this area of study is not assessed in the course assignment.

Of course, you will be assessed on the content of the Computer Systems area of study in the exam.

Course Assessment Structure
Component 1   Exam Paper: 110 marks
Component 2   Assignment: 50 marks
Total: **160 marks**

THE ASSIGNMENT

The assignment is set by the SQA on an annual basis and sent off to be externally marked.

It is made up of three separate tasks. The marks are allocated across three areas of study, which are covered by the assignment as follows:

Software Design and Development   (25 marks)
Database Design and Development   (10–15 marks)
Web Design and Development   (10–15 marks)

The purpose of the assignment is to assess your ability to produce a solution to an appropriate computing problem that is based upon the knowledge and skills that you have developed during this course. It is set by the SQA and carried out under controlled conditions. This is an open-book assessment, which means that you can look over programs, websites and database software that you have previously written to refresh your memory on particular skills that you may have forgotten. You can use manuals and textbooks to obtain more information and extend your skills.

Your teacher is not allowed to give you any help or advice to perform this task. You are expected to show your own initiative in this task and to persevere with a problem in the search for a solution.

The assignment is not just about finding a practical solution at the computer. It involves analysing a problem, designing a solution, implementing the solution and then testing and evaluating the solution. The necessary skills to address these stages should have been covered in your class work and are described in the topics in this book. The assignment is broken down into a series of short tasks which guide you in clear stages through the assessment.

DON'T FORGET

A specimen assignment is available which will give you an indication of the level of difficulty and style of practical tasks that you can expect in the actual course assignment.

MARKS

The marks are not just for the practical work that you do on the computer.

Most of the marks are for the practical implementation and testing of your solution, but a lot of the marks are for the analysis, design and evaluation.

The marks for the assignment are spread across five development skills as follows:

Analysis   (5 marks)
Design   (5 marks)
Implementation   (30 marks)
Testing   (5 marks)
Evaluation   (5 marks)

THE REPORT

You report on the solution by competing a word-processed report which covers the stages of analysis, design, implementation, testing and evaluation.

Your teacher will give you a template word-processing document with questions and spaces for you to enter your answers.

People are impressed by appearances, so don't let your good practical work down by handing in a report that is difficult to read. Format the text in your report in a font and font size that is easy to read.

EVIDENCE CHECKLIST

A checklist is provided with your instructions which details all of the evidence that you must gather while performing this task. You must submit this evidence for this part of the task to your teacher.

The checklist is there to help you to make sure that you have included all of the necessary items in your report before you hand it in.

The checklist covers each stage of the assignment tasks such as evidence of test runs, database reports, website pages, CSS code and so on.

The completed report document and the supporting evidence must be printed out so that it can be sent to the SQA in paper-based format.

 THINGS TO DO AND THINK ABOUT

It cannot be overstressed that the software solutions for the assignment only make up 60% of the total marks.

Make sure that you carefully read every word of the assignment and meet all of the requirements of the documentation write-up for analysis, design, testing and evaluation to gain your best possible mark.

 **DON'T FORGET**

It is a common fault for students to concentrate solely on producing the practical solution for the assignment and not to put the same effort into the documentation of the solution. Make sure that you put the same effort into the analysis, design, testing and evaluation as you do into the implemented solution.

 ONLINE

You can find lots more details of course assessment for the Higher course on the Scottish Qualifications Authority website at www.sqa.org.uk/sqa/56924.html

APPENDICES

ANSWERS

SOFTWARE DESIGN AND DEVELOPMENT

REVISION QUESTIONS 1

Answer 1

(a) Robust.

(b) Agile.

(c) Fit for purpose.

(d) Maintainable.

(e) Efficient.

Answer 2

(a) The score must be entered until it satisfies the complex condition
Score >=0 AND Score <= 6.
The number of times that the loop is repeated is not fixed but is repeated until a condition is true.

(b) A function.
This subroutine is a function, since it returns a single value.
A procedure is used to create an effect such as sorting a list or entering a set of data.

(c) (i) The integer data type cannot store decimal fractions such as 5·3, since it only stores positive and negative whole numbers, plus zero.
REAL would be a suitable data type, since it can store decimal fractions as well as whole numbers.

(ii) The parameter should be passed by reference. An array is always passed by reference, since passing it by value would require a copy to be made of a large amount of data.

(d) (i) Maintenance would be easier, since the data is manipulated as a unit, so that changes to the program can be effected much more quickly than by modifying six independent variables.

(ii) The program would be more efficient, since the data in the array can be manipulated in a loop rather than needing to process each variable with separate instructions, which would be required for the six variables.

(iii) There would be no change to the storage requirements, since ten items of data are being stored in each method.

(e) The algorithm is shown below with lines 12, 18 and 20 completed.

```
1   SET Scores TO [5·2, 5·5, 4·9, 5·2, 5·7, 5·3]
2   SET Position TO 0
3   SET Min TO Scores[Position]
4   FOR Position FROM 1 TO 5 DO
5       IF Scores[Position] < Min THEN
6           SET Min TO Scores[Position]
7       END IF
8   END FOR
9   SET Position TO 0
10  SET Max TO Score[Position]
11  FOR Position FROM 1 TO 5 DO
12      IF Scores[Position] > Max THEN
13          SET Max TO Scores[Position]
14      END IF
15  END FOR
16  SET Total TO 0
17  FOR Position FROM 0 TO 5 DO
18      SET Total TO Total + Scores[Position]
19  END FOR
20  SET Overall TO Total – Max – Min
21  SEND ["The overall score is: ", Overall] TO DISPLAY
```

Answer 3

(a) Record Oscar IS {INTEGER Year, STRING Category, STRING Winner, STRING Film}

(b) Declare Oscars(2946) AS ARRAY OF Oscar

(c) The algorithm is illustrated in SQA reference language.

```
SET Count TO 0
RECEIVE SearchFilm from KEYBOARD
FOR Index FROM 0 TO 2946 DO
    IF Oscars[Index].Film = SearchFilm THEN
        SET Count TO Count + 1
    END IF
END FOR
SEND ["Number of Oscars won: ", SearchFilm]
TO DISPLAY
```

Note: There is more than one answer to this question, but it should follow the counting-occurrences standard algorithm as shown above.

contd

REVISION QUESTIONS 2

Answer 1

(a) A data type defines how an item of data is represented in memory, and restricts the operations that can be performed on the data.
Note: For example, if a variable is declared as a String data type, then operations such as finding the square root are not allowed, since you can't find the square root of a piece of text such as "Wyoming"!

(ii) An array data structure.
The names would be stored in the STRING data type.

(b) (i) Counting occurrences

(ii) Finding minimum.

(c) An example of a solution is shown below. Your own algorithm does not need to be identical but should follow the same logical steps.

```
1   Set Counter TO 0
2   FOR Position FROM 0 TO 79 DO
3   IF Time[Position] < 12 THEN
4        SET Counter TO Counter + 1
5   END IF
6   END FOR
7   SEND ["The number of star awards is: ", Counter]
    TO DISPLAY
```

(d) (i) Global variables can be assigned a value throughout the entire program, so that any changes to them in one subprogram can have an impact on other subprograms, which is poor for module independence.
This can be overcome with the use of local variables, which are declared within a subprogram and only exist within the subprogram, thus improving the independence of the module.

(ii) Independent modules make it easier to modify and maintain software, since any changes to a module have no effect on the rest of the program, thus saving time in checking through other subprograms.

Answer 2

(a) The programmers would be biased in not being alert to the presence of errors.
Also, the independent test group would be experienced in locating errors.

(b) Test data 1:   10, 20, 24, 5, 14, 2
Reason for choice: To test whether the program can give correct results for normal data.

Test data 2:   0, 12, 13, 22, 23, 25
Reason for choice: To test whether the program can give correct results for extreme data.

Test data 3:   27, –3, 144, A, Polly, K9
Reason for choice: To test whether the program can cope with exceptions without crashing or giving incorrect results.

(c) Test data 1
Expected output: 3 fails, 2 passes, 1 pass with distinction.

Test data 2
Expected output: 2 fails, 2 passes, 2 passes with distinction.

Test data 3
Expected output: The program should return an error message and ask for the data to be re-entered.

Answer 3

(a) The completed table is shown below.

	MaxPopulation	Index	MaxCountry
Line 1	32268240		
Line 2		1	
Line 4			France
Line 2		2	
Line 4			Japan
Line 2		3	
Line 4			Italy
Line 2		4	
Line 4			Italy

(b) When Index = 1, then the IF statement is True, and MaxCountry is assigned to CountryList[1], which is "France".
However, when Position = 3, the IF statement is True, and MaxCountry is assigned to CountryList [3], which is "Italy", giving the wrong result.
This is because the MaxPopulation variable is set to the first item in the PopulationList array and never changes. Any item in the PopulationList array that is greater than the first item will make the IF statement TRUE even if there are previous items that are greater than the current item.
The algorithm will result in the MaxCountry variable being set to the last item in the list that has a population greater than the first item, and not the maximum value in the entire list.
An example of a correct algorithm is given below, but there is more than one solution.
This algorithm works by inserting an extra line (LINE 5), which updates the value of MaxPopulation each time a higher population is found.

```
LINE 1    SET MaxPopulation TO PopulationList[0]
LINE 2    FOR Index FROM 1 TO SizeofList – 1
LINE 3        IF PopulationList[Index] >
MaxPopulation THEN
LINE 4            SET MaxCountry TO
CountryList[Index]
LINE 5            SET MaxPopulation TO
Population[Index]
LINE 6        END IF
LINE 7    END FOR
LINE 8    SEND [MaxCountry] TO DISPLAY
```

COMPUTER SYSTEMS

REVISION QUESTIONS 1

Answer 1

(a) Standards allow text, numbers etc. to be transferred between different programs and be interpreted as the same value without the need for conversion.
If different programs represented data differently, then the data could not be transferred between programs without conversion.

(b) $2^{32} - 1 = 4,294,967,295$.
There are 2^{32} different numbers that can be represented in 32 bits.
The largest number is 1 less than 2^{32}, since the smallest number is zero.

(c) $2^{15} - 1 = 32,767$.
The largest positive number in 16-bit two's complement will start with a 0 and then have fifteen 1s.
There are 2^{15} different numbers that can be represented in 15 bits.
The largest number is 1 less than 2^{15}, since the smallest number is zero.

(d) "Real" is better, because an 8-bit mantissa would provide sufficient accuracy, and an 8-bit exponent would provide a sufficient range of numbers.
Since the numbers only require an accuracy of 2 decimal places and are relatively small, using "Surreal" would use more bits for storage than is required in this situation and would not be efficient.
"Surreal" would provide more accuracy and a larger range of numbers, but this is not required for numbers such as 10·03, 9·98 etc. and would needlessly increase the storage requirements of the data.

(e) Extended ASCII uses less storage than Unicode, since each character is coded in 8 bits compared to Unicode's 16 bits.
Unicode can represent 2^{16} characters (65,536), whereas Extended ASCII can only represent 28 characters (256).

(f) The image is stored as a list of objects (Rectangle, Circle, Line) and their attributes.

Answer 2

(a) (i) A resolution of 100 dpi would be too low for a catalogue, because the images would be blurred and grainy-looking.

(ii) A higher resolution such as 600 dpi would be more suitable, since the images would be clearer and of better quality.

The disadvantage is that the images would have much higher storage requirements.

(b) A vector graphics package stores an image by objects and their attributes, which would not be able to create the detail required for the gnomes, which are too complex to be represented by simply using circles, lines and so on.

(c) Standard file formats for graphics include: GIF, JPEG, PNG etc.

(d) True colour has a bit depth of 24 bits.
The increase from 16 bits to 24 bits will increase the storage requirements by a factor of 50%.

Answer 3

(a) Step 1
The processor sets up the address bus with the address of the memory location holding the instruction.

Step 2
The processor activates the READ line on the control bus.

Step 3
The instruction is transferred along the data bus into the instruction register in the processor.

Step 4
The instruction is decoded and executed.

(b) (i) The control bus is a collection of lines that are used individually to send and receive signals to initiate events, whereas the data and address bus are used as a group of lines to encode an item of data or an address.

(ii) Read – A signal used to initiate a memory READ operation
Write – A signal used to initiate a memory WRITE operation
Clock – A regular series of pulses into the processor to synchronise events
Reset – A signal that causes the computer to stop execution of the current program and reboot.

(c) (i) Cache improves processor performance by keeping frequently held instructions and data in memory on the processor chip itself or in fast-access memory.

(ii) Increasing the clock speed will improve the processor performance by increasing the number of read/write cycles per second.
Increasing the width of the data bus will improve the processor performance by increasing the number of bits that are processed in each cycle.

contd

REVISION QUESTIONS 2

Answer 1

(a) Two's complement is used to represent integer numbers, which are positive and negative whole numbers and zero.
Floating-point notation stores real numbers, which are all numbers including decimal fractions.

(b) The 8-bit two's complement answers are:

   (i) 01010001

   (ii) 11100111

(c) 8,571

(d) 1000011101010101

Answer 2

(a) (i) Encryption is used to encode the message.
A combination of public and private keys is used to encode and decode the data.
The customer uses a public key to encrypt the data; then a private key is used by the company to decrypt the data.

   (ii) A digital certificate includes:

- the user's name

- the name of the organisation that issued the certificate (the Certificate Authority)

- the user's e-mail address

- the user's public key.

   (iii) A digital signature can be attached to a message which uniquely identifies the sender and therefore guarantees that the message is from the person it claims
to be from.
The company can use its private key to attach a digital signature to the message being transmitted. Once the message is received, then the customer's public key is used to decrypt the digital signature. The public key is paired with the private key so that the customer is sure that it must be the company that sent the message.

(b) (i) Intelligent traffic-control systems can have a positive environmental impact by:

- monitoring traffic flow, weather and road conditions to always take the most efficient (in terms of energy) route to the destination

- self-driving cars, which can be programmed to go at an optimum speed to minimise fuel consumption.

   (ii) A negative impact of the traffic-control system could be:

- Energy is required to manufacture and run the sensors and cameras and other hardware that are used by intelligent traffic-control systems.

- Other suitable answers are possible.

Answer 3

(a) The Computer Misuse Act.

(b) (i) A tracking cookie is a text file that is stored on the user's computer which contains data to remember the user's activities when visiting a website.
It stores data such as usernames and passwords so that you do not have to sign in again every time you return to a website.

   (ii) The students might be concerned that cookies are an invasion of their privacy or a security risk.
For example, hackers can obtain confidential information such as logon details that a cookie saves, and browsing habits can be obtained which can be sold to companies who can then flood the user with unwanted junk email.

(c) (i) Denial of Service.

   (ii) Types of DoS attack include:

- bandwidth consumption, which uses up the available bandwidth by sending the server a large number of data packets in a short period of time, so that the server grinds to a halt.

- resource starvation, which consumes the system's resources such as the server's hard-disc space by sending a large volume of data.

- Domain Name Service (DNS) attack, which sends a large number of DNS queries with a false IP address of the target server to a DNS server. The DNS server then floods the target server with an excessive number of replies.

   (iii) A DoS attack can be costly to an organisation for several reasons:

- The loss of business during the attack downtime

- The cost of repair and response to the attack

- Loss of confidence by users in the organisation.

   (iv) Denial-of-Service attacks are sometimes carried out by organisations for financial and political reasons to gain an advantage over their competitors.
Individuals carry out DoS attacks for personal reasons, such as by a disgruntled employee who has been sacked and wants to mount an attack against the organisation that sacked him/her.

DATABASE DESIGN AND DEVELOPMENT

REVISION QUESTIONS 1

Answer 1

(a) The primary key in the Actor table is Actor ID.
The foreign key in the Actor table is Agent ID.

(b) Any two of the following are examples of one-to-many relationships:
Agent and Actor (one record in the Agent table can appear many times in the Actor table, since one agent can manage many actors).
Actor and Film (one record in the Actor table can appear many times in the Film table, since one actor can have appeared in many films).
Studio and Film (one record in the Studio table can appear many times in the Film table, since one studio can have made many films).

(c) (i) The Sex (M/F) fields could be made Boolean field types, making it more intuitive to click on a Male or Female option button.
A restricted-choice option could be used for the actor's date-of-birth field by using a date-picker calendar to select the date, rather than the user typing the date in, which could lead to errors.

(ii) The actor's age is not included in the entry form because it can be calculated automatically from the actor's date-of-birth field and today's date, using a formula in a calculated field.

(d) A query can be created which is illustrated by the following design:

Field(s) and calculation(s)	Actor.Actor name, Actor.Actor photo, Actor.Actor age, Agent.Agent telephone number
Table(s) and query	Studio
Search criteria	Studio.Studio name = "3D Flicks"
Grouping	
Sort order	

A report can then be created using the data from the query.

Answer 2

The tables below show suitable values for the answers A to L.

There are other possible answers, since there are issues such as the validation used for the length of the author's name, which of course is subjective.
If you are not sure, ask your teacher.

Entity name: Author				
Attribute	**Key**	**Type**	**Unique**	**Validation**
authorID	PK	NUMBER	Y	>=1 and <= 999
name		TEXT	N	**Max length = 30**
sex		TEXT	N	Restricted choice (F, M)
email		TEXT	Y	Max length = 30

Entity name: Book				
Attribute	**Key**	**Type**	**Unique**	**>=1 and <=999**
bookID	PK	NUMBER	Y	>=1 and <= 9,999
authorID*	**FK**	NUMBER	N	**Lookup from Author table**
title		TEXT	N	Max length = 40
hardback		BOOLEAN	N	**Restricted choice (Y, N)**
genre		TEXT	N	Max length = 40
publisher		TEXT	N	**Max length = 30**
publicationdate		DATE	N	**Restricted choice (date-picker)**

contd

Answer 3

(a) Cardinality defines the type of relationship between two entities by stating the number of entity occurrences in one entity that are associated with one occurrence of the related entity.
Cardinality can be one-to-one, one-to-many or many-to-many.

(b) Each relationship is explained below.

A   Actors, and films that they have appeared in, is a many-to-many relationship.
An actor can appear in many films, and a film can have many actors in it.

B   Headteachers, and schools that they manage, is a one-to-one relationship.
One headteacher can be associated with only one school, and one school can only have one headteacher.

C   Mothers and their children are a one-to-many relationship.
One mother can have many children, but one child will only have one mother.

D   Athletes, and events in a sporting competition, is a many-to-many relationship.
An athlete can enter more than one event, and an event will have many athletes.

E   Capital cities, and countries in the world, is a one-to-one relationship.
One capital city is linked to one country, and one country has only one capital city.

(c) A many-to-many relationship is resolved by forming two one-to-many relationships.

(d) An entity-relationship diagram illustrates a model of the types of relationship between the entities in a relational database, whereas an entity-occurrence diagram illustrates instances of specific examples of entity relationships. For example, John Higgins is linked to High Jump, Javelin and 1500m.

REVISION QUESTIONS 2

Answer 1

(a) (i) The population field of the "Wood pigeon" record would be changed from "decreasing" to "stable".

(ii) A new record would be added to the table for an "Eagle", which has a clutch size of 2 and where the population is stable.

(iii) The records for Blackbird, Magpie and Wren would be removed from the table.

(b) (i)

birds	
name	clutch_size
Robin	5
Blackbird	6
Magpie	6
Blue tit	5
Swan	5

(ii)

birds		
name	clutch_size	population
Chaffinch	4	increasing
Goldfinch	4	stable
Thrush	3	decreasing

Answer 2

(a) (i) Wildcard characters are used to search a string where some of the characters are known and the rest of the characters may be anything.
e.g. searching for a name that starts with "Mac".

(ii) SQL uses a percentage character to represent a wildcard that is zero, one or many characters, and an underscore character to represent a single wildcard character.

(b) (i) The code selects the names of all the countries which end in the letters "ya".
The "%" character means that the country's name can start with any string of characters so long as it ends with the characters "ya".

(ii) The code selects the names of all the countries whose second letter is "g".
The "_" character means that the country's name can start with any single character so long as the second character is a "g", and the remaining part of the country's name can be any string of characters.

(c) The AS keyword is used as an alias which exists temporarily during the execution of the query.
Its purpose is to make the columns selected more readable by using "Pet" and "Species" for field names instead of "pet_id" and "pet_species".

contd

ANSWERS

Answer 3

(a) (i) Aggregate functions group the values of multiple rows together and calculate a single value on each group, such as the highest or the average value.

(ii) Examples of aggregate functions include COUNT, SUM, MAX, MIN, AVG.
There are other aggregate functions such as MEDIAN which would be suitable for this answer, but the ones listed above are those that you are expected to know for this course.

(b) The tables below show the results table for each query. It is important that you give the table heading as well as the actual results data.

(i)

MIN(english)
43

(ii)

sex	MAX(art)
M	90
F	87

(iii)

sex	COUNT(name)
F	6
M	7

(iv)

sex	AVG(maths)
F	68
M	66

WEB DESIGN AND DEVELOPMENT

REVISION QUESTIONS 1

Answer 1

(a) Visual layout.
The visual layout should be clear and uncluttered so that it is not confusing to a young child. For example, it could have large images to click on, and could split the screen into coloured panels to clearly indicate different sections.
The readability should reflect the reading age of the users and should use simple short words in a large and attractive font to indicate actions.

(b) Creating the wireframe designs means that the developers can obtain early feedback from the teachers on the suitability of the interface for the children and can make any necessary amendments.

(c) (i) The usability would be poor for five-year-old children since they would find it difficult to navigate through a series of menus and sub-menus.

(ii) A simpler structure that uses one level, or maybe just one sub-level, could be used.

(d) There can be compatibility problems with browsers. Even if the website works correctly on Firefox, it does not mean that it will necessarily work on a different browser in the school.
For example, media file formats are not supported by all browsers, and they might not display properly.

(e) Just because the teachers find the website usable does not mean that the five-year-old children will find it easy to use.
The website should be further tested by the pupils themselves to see if it is fit for purpose for the end users.

Answer 2

(a) All of the links in the navigation bars should be tested to see if they go to their intended target without error.
Input into text boxes should be tested to verify that any validation-checks work correctly, such as range- or length-check.
Media elements such as graphics, video etc. should all be tested to ensure that they display or play correctly.

(b) Only testing the website on a desktop computer is inadequate, because it has not been checked to see if the website displays and functions correctly on other types of device, such as tablet computers and smartphones.
The developers need to test the website on different types of device to check whether the website displays properly on different screen sizes and at different aspect ratios and so on.

(c) Not all browsers are the same, and the website must be tested to see whether it works correctly with the range of browsers for its intended use, and not just on Google Chrome.

(d) Not all browsers support the wide variety of file formats that are available for media, so media file formats should be chosen that are compatible with the browsers that will be used for the website.

contd

90

Answer 3

(a) (i) The term "usability" means how easy it is for a user to interact with the interface in terms of the speed of performing tasks and at a low error rate.

(ii) This is a good usability feature, because the user only has to enter a few characters, and the predictive text will suggest a valid airport which the user can then select with the mouse. This will reduce the time taken to enter the data and will eliminate the entering of invalid data.

(b) The user can only select valid data and not enter data that does not exist or is in the past, in the wrong format and so on.

The data can be entered more quickly than by typing the date with the keyboard.

(c) The entering of the class (economy, business, first) could be achieved by using restricted choices in which the user selects a class from a drop-down list. This would remove any chance of invalid input and be quick and easy to perform.

(d) The developers can carry out usability testing by giving users a series of tasks to perform. They can monitor the time taken to complete these tasks and the error rate.
They could also have discussions with the users to gain feedback on what tasks the users found difficult to perform and on how the interface could be improved.

REVISION QUESTIONS 2

Answer 1

(a) Grouping selectors allow CSS rules to be set for more than one selector at the same time.

```
e.g.    h1, h2, p {
        text-align: center;
        color: red;
        }
```

Descendant selectors allow CSS rules to be set for a descendant of an ancestor selector that match the CSS rules of the ancestor.

```
e.g.    div p {
        font-size: 18px;
        background-color: yellow;
        }
```

(b) Using grouping and descendant selectors makes a website easier to maintain, since the CSS rules can be changed for more than one element at the same time.

Answer 2

(a) Completed code:

```
<input type="text" name="student" size="30" maxlength="25" required>
```

(b) A "text" input type is used to enter a single line of text, where a "textarea" input type is used to enter text into a box that can have multiple lines.

(c) Select country:

```
<select name="country">
<option value="England">England</option>
<option value="Northern Ireland">Northern Ireland</option>
<option value="Scotland">Scotland</option>
<option value="Wales">Wales</option>
</select>
```

(d) The code to enter the student's age:

```
<input type="number" name="age" min="12" max="18" required>
```

(e) The code to enter the student's chess standard:

```
<input type="radio" name="standard" value="Beginner"> Beginner
<input type="radio" name="standard" value="Intermediate"> Intermediate
<input type="radio" name="standard" value="Advanced"> Advanced
```

(f) When the student clicks on the "Submit" button, the form data is processed by a server-side script.

The browser will show any validation errors which must be corrected by the user before the form can be submitted.

Answer 3

(a) Completed code:

```
.invisible{display: none;}
```

(b) Completed code:

```
<p id="visible" class="invisible">Ninety legs.</p>
```

GLOSSARY

Address bus – A processor bus that is used to specify which memory location is to be used to read data from or to write data to.

Aggregate function –A database function that is used to perform calculations involving multiple records.

Agile methodologies –A software-development methodology that stresses flexibility, adaptability, collaboration and client feedback.

Alias –A database keyword that temporarily renames a field selected by an SQL statement to make it more readable.

ALU (Arithmetic Logic Unit) –A component of the processor that performs arithmetic operations and logical decisions.

Array –A data structure that stores a list of items of the same data type.

AVG –An aggregate function that calculates an average of multiple records.

Bit-mapped graphics –A graphic where the image is stored as a binary code for the colour of pixels.

BMP (Bitmap) –A standard file format for graphics that uses a binary code to store the colour of each pixel.

Boolean –A data type used for a variable that is storing only the values True or False.

Boolean field –A database field that stores only two values (Yes or No).

Boundaries –A specification of the limits that define what is in a software project and what is not.

Breakpoint –A marker that is set in a program that suspends the execution of the program at that point so that the contents of the variables in the program can then be examined.

Browser –A program that displays web pages and is used to navigate the internet.

Cache memory –An area of fast-access memory that stores frequently used instructions and data.

Carbon footprint –A measure of how much carbon dioxide is produced in the making and use of computing equipment.

Central Processing Unit (CPU) –The part of a computer that executes programs, which consists of a processor chip and main memory chips.

Character –A data type used for a variable that is storing a single character.

Clear (both) –A CSS property that floats elements on the left or the right side of a specified element.

Clock speed –The time interval between regular pulses into the processor which synchronise events.

Compatibility testing –Testing a website to ensure that it works in the same way across a range of platforms.

Compound key –A type of primary key which uses a combination of two or more attributes to identify a record uniquely.

Computer Misuse Act 1990 –A law that makes it illegal to gain unauthorised access to computer data with the intent to commit a further offence or to modify the data.

Control bus –A processor bus that has a series of lines that are used to send out signals to initiate events.

Control unit –A component of the processor that manages the fetching and execution of instructions from main memory.

Cookie –A text file that is used to store data on a user's computer to remember the user's activities when visiting a website.

Core –One of several processor components which can independently execute program instructions.

COUNT –An aggregate function that performs a count of multiple records.

Counting occurrences –A standard algorithm that counts the number of items in a list that meet certain criteria.

CSS (Cascading Style Sheets) –A system for defining the way a web page is formatted by using CSS rules to define the font, colour, size and alignment of text, the positions of images etc.

CSV (Comma-Separated Values) –A text-file format that can be used to save tabular data such as spreadsheets by using symbols to separate the rows and columns.

Data bus –A processor bus that is used to carry data from a memory location to the processor and vice versa.

Data dictionary –A table used in database design that details the properties of the tables and fields.

Data flow –The data and how it must flow in or out of the subprograms in a program.

Data types –Different kinds of data stored by a variable in a program, such as Integer, String, Boolean etc.

Date field –A database field that stores a date.

DELETE –A SQL statement that is used to remove a record from a table.

Denial-of-service attack –An attack on a company's network that puts it under pressure in a way that prevents legitimate users from being able to use the network resources.

Descendant selector –A CSS selector that matches all elements that are descendants of a specified element.

Digital certificate –An electronic document issued by a Certificate Authority that contains the public key for a digital signature and specifies the identity associated with the key, such as the name of an organisation.

Digital signature –A digital code that is attached to an electronically transmitted document to verify its contents and the sender's identity.

Display (block, inline, none) –A CSS property that specifies how an element is displayed.

Dry run –A technique that involves stepping through the program instructions and manually working out how the program variables are updated.

Efficiency –A feature of software whereby the amount of code or speed of execution are in proportion to the scale of the problem.

Encryption –Encoding data so that it cannot be interpreted if unlawfully accessed.

End user –The person/persons who will be using an item of software once it has been developed.

Entity-occurrence diagram –A diagram used in database design that illustrates specific relationships between entities by giving instances of actual occurrences.

Entity-relationship diagram –A diagram that represents the relationship between tables in a relational database by showing the links between the primary and foreign keys.

Exceptional data –A set of test data that is chosen to test whether the software can deal with unexpected data without crashing.

Execution errors –Errors that are detected during the running of the program, such as trying to divide by zero.

Exponent –The power part of a floating-point number.

Extended ASCII –American Standard Code for Information Interchange: a system for storing characters on a computer system using an 8-bit code.

External stylesheet –CSS rules that are defined in a separate .CSS file with a link placed in the <head> section of the HTML document.

Extreme data –A set of test data that is chosen to test that the software can handle data which lies on the boundaries of possible inputs.

Fetch–execute cycle –The mechanism a computer uses to solve a problem by storing a set of instructions in memory that are then fetched and executed one at a time.

Field-length check –A validation check which forces the entered data to be a specified number of characters long.

Finding maximum –A standard algorithm that finds the highest value in a list of items.

Finding minimum –A standard algorithm that finds the lowest value in a list of items.

Fitness for purpose –Software that fulfils the requirements and does what it is supposed to do.

Float (left, right) –A CSS property that specifies whether an element is to be floated to the left or right.

Floating-point notation –A system for storing real numbers on a computer system.

Flowchart –A method of design that represents an algorithm by showing the steps as boxes of various kinds, and their order by connecting them with arrows.

Footer (HTML) –An HTML tag that represents a container for the end of a document.

Foreign key –An attribute of an entity that contains occurrences that correspond to occurrences in the primary key of another entity.

Form (HTML) –An HTML tag that defines a form that is used to collect user input.

Function –A subprogram that returns a single value.

Functional requirements –The input, processing and output operations that a computer system is required to perform.

GIF (Graphics Interchange Format) –A standard file format for graphics that uses lossless compression and represents 256 colours.

Global variable –A variable that is recognised throughout the whole program.

GROUP BY –SQL keywords that are used to group records together to provide calculations on groups of records in a column.

Grouping selector –A CSS selector that is used to specify the same properties and rules for more than one HTML element at the same time.

Header (HTML) –An HTML tag that represents a container for the start of a document.

Hover –A CSS selector which is used to select and style an HTML element when the mouse hovers over it.

HTML (Hypertext Mark-up Language) –A language that uses a list of tags to describe the page's format and what is displayed on the web page.

ID attribute (HTML) –A CSS selector that is used to select one unique HTML element.

Input validation –The process of repeatedly asking for an item of data to be entered until it is within its possible range of values.

INSERT –A SQL statement that is used to add a new record to a table.

Integer –A data type used for a variable that is storing a positive or negative whole number.

Intelligent system –An artificial-intelligence system that gathers and analyses data, adapts to changing circumstances and learns from previous experience.

Internal stylesheet –CSS rules that are defined within a <style> element in the <head> section of a page.

Iterative development –A software-development process which proceeds through a series of phases, with phases being revisited in light of experience gained at a later stage.

JavaScript –A programming language that can be incorporated into web pages to add interactivity and make them more dynamic.

JPEG (Joint Photographic Enterprise Group) –A standard file format for graphics that uses lossy compression and represents over 16 million colours.

Linear search –A standard algorithm that searches for a value at the first item in a list and continues searching through each item of the list in turn.

List-style-type: none –A CSS property that specifies the type of list-item marker in a list.

Local variable –A variable that is only recognised in the subprogram in which it is declared.

Logical errors –Errors caused by mistakes in the code that cause the program not to produce the correct results.

Lossless compression –File compression that results in no reduction in quality.

Lossy compression –File compression that reduces the quality of the file.

Machine code –The computer's own programming language, where instructions and data are written in binary codes.

Main (HTML) –An HTML tag that represents a container for the main content of a document.

Maintainability –How easy it is to make modifications to software at a later stage.

Mantissa –The fractional part of a floating-point number which stores the significant figures of the number.

Many-to-many relationship –A relationship between two tables in a database in which one record in a table is associated with multiple records in a second table and vice versa.

Margins –A CSS property that specifies the amount of space around elements, outside of any defined borders.

MAX –An aggregate function that returns the highest value of multiple records.

MIN –An aggregate function that returns the lowest value of multiple records.

Modulus –An operator that returns the remainder after a number is divided by a divisor.

MP3 (MPEG Layer 3) –A standard file format for sound that uses lossy compression so that the quality is reduced.

MP4 (Motion Picture Experts Group) –A standard file format for video that uses lossy compression.

Multi-level website –A website where the home page is at the top, and it breaks underneath into categories which can be further broken into sub-categories.

Nav (HTML) –An HTML tag that is used define a set of navigation links.

Navigation bar –A set of buttons or images in a row or column that provides links to various sections of a website.

Normal data –A set of test data that is chosen to test that the software gives correct results for everyday data.

Number element (HTML form) –An input element for an HTML form that is used to enter a number.

Number field –A database field that stores a number.

Onclick –A mouse event which triggers the execution of code when a button or other element is clicked.

One-to-many relationship –A relationship between two tables in a database in which one record in a table is associated with multiple records in a second table.

One-to-one relationship –A relationship between two tables in a database in which one record in a table is associated with one record in a second table.

Onmouseout –A mouse event which triggers the execution of code when the mouse pointer is moved away from a specified element in a web page.

Onmouseover –A mouse event which triggers the execution of code when the mouse pointer is moved over a specified element in a web page.

ORDER BY –SQL keywords that are used to sort records in ascending or descending order.

Parameter –A parameter is a variable or value that is passed into and/or out of a subprogram.

PNG (Portable Network Graphics) –A standard file format for graphics that uses lossless compression and represents over 16 million colours.

Pre-defined function –A function built into the programming language which performs mathematical calculations, manipulates text etc.

Presence-check –A validation check that is used to stop important data from being missed out and that will not allow a field to be left blank.

Primary key –An attribute or combination of attributes that uniquely identifies one, and only one, entity occurrence.

Private key –An encryption key that is held privately by the recipient of encrypted data that is used to sign digital signatures and to decrypt data that was encoded using the recipient's public key.

Procedure –A subprogram that produces an effect.

Prototype –A small-scale version of a website or software which can be used to get feedback from the end users before the full-scale project is developed.

Pseudocode –A method of design that uses natural language to represent the detailed logic of the program code.

Public key –An encryption key that can be obtained and used by anyone to encrypt messages intended for a particular recipient.

Purpose –A general description of what the software is to be used for.

Query –A request for data from one or more database tables.

Radio element (HTML form) –An input element for an HTML form that is used to select **one** of a limited number of choices.

Range-check –A validation check which forces the entered data to lie in a certain range of values.

Real –A data type used for a variable that is storing a positive or negative decimal number.

Record (programming language) –A data structure which can store variables of different data types in fields.

Registers –Individual storage locations on the processor that store single items of data.

Relative hyperlink –A relative hyperlink uses a path from the current page to the destination page.

Example: <a href="weather.html">Click here</a>

Restricted choice –A validation check that limits what the user can enter by restricting the choice to a list of acceptable values.

Robust –Describes software that does not crash easily with unexpected input.

Scope –A list of the items that the development of a software project must cover, such as the completed program, test runs and the time limit for the project.

Scripting language –A language that operates alongside an application package and allows the user to customise the package and to automate tasks.

Section (HTML) –An HTML tag that defines a section in a document such as a chapter, header, footer etc.

Select element (HTML form) –An input element for an HTML form that is used to create a drop-down list.

Sequential file –A text file that stores items of data one after another and is terminated with an end-of-file (EOF) marker.

Sizes (height, width) –CSS properties that specify the height and width of an element.

SQL –A programming language that is used to manage the data in a database by selecting, updating, inserting and deleting data.

Standard algorithms –Common algorithms that are used in programs over and over again.

Standard file format –Commonly used file formats for text, graphics, video and audio files.

Stepwise refinement –A series of steps in which a large problem is broken down into parts and then those parts themselves are further broken down into smaller parts.

String –A data type used for a variable that is storing an item of text.

Structure diagram –A method of design that splits a program up into successively smaller, more manageable parts in a hierarchical structure.

Submit element (HTML form) –A button that is used for submitting the form data to a form-handler, which is typically a server page with a script for processing input data.

Subprogram –A block of code (function or procedure) that is created and then evoked with a single command.

Substring –A function that returns part of a string.

SUM –An aggregate function that calculates the total of values in multiple records.

Syntax errors –Errors which result from mistakes in the instructions of a programming language.

Text element (HTML form) –An input element for an HTML form that is used to enter an item of text.

Text field –A database field that stores a string of characters.

Textarea element (HTML form) –An input element for an HTML form that is used to enter an item of text that can span several lines.

Time field –A database field that stores a time of day.

Top-level design –The first breakdown of a program into its major steps.

Trace table –A table that is used to manually step through a program line by line while watching how variables are updated after each instruction has been executed.

Two's complement –A system for storing integers on a computer system.

TXT (text) –A standard file format for text that stores no formatting information.

Unicode –A standard code for storing characters that uses 16 bits.

UPDATE –A SQL statement that is used to amend a record in a table.

Usability –Describes how easily the user can use a program by performing actions quickly and without errors.

Usability testing –Testing how quickly and error-free the end users can use the software interface to navigate and perform given tasks.

User interface –Describes how the user communicates with a computer program.

Vector graphics –A graphic where the image is stored as a list of objects and their attributes.

Watchpoint –A conditional breakpoint that halts program execution when a condition is met, such as a variable being less than a certain value.

WAV (Waveform Audio Format) –A standard file format for sound that uses lossless compression.

WHERE –A SQL statement that is used to set the criteria for a SELECT statement.

White space –Blank areas in the program listing, such as blank lines between control constructs and procedures, and indentation in loops and IFs.

Wildcard –A symbol that is used as a substitute for no/one/more character(s) in a string.

Wireframe –A skeletal illustration of a user interface showing the positioning of elements on the screen.

INDEX